Ellipsis

• • •

Nancy Schellinger Rhode
and
Nicki Rhode Peasley

This book belongs to Love.

•••

ISBN-13: 978-1720399193
ISBN-10: 1720399190

Cover Photograph: Jodi Bock
Cover Design and Illustrations: suzanne l. vinson
suzannelvinson.com

Thank you for your vision, dear friends.

And thank you to my first readers, Faith Grieger and Julie Hulett,
for encouraging me to put these words in the world...

● ● ●

Ellipsis: an indication of pause or wavering, allowing space for breath, for reflection, for mystery; an intentional omission that invites the reader to complete the circle...

.

Dedication

For All of Us...

Stories are expressions of the human mind, thus no story is
absolutely true.
Truth is multidimensional.
My truth abides in the vibration around these words... in the
circle of memory, imagination, and Divine inspiration.

Preface

•••

My mom passed away on December 19, 2015. And she is the co-author of this book, *her words distinguished by italics*. These pages hold a conversation between mother and daughter that transcends human roles and, hopefully, sparks synergy among souls. This project is proof that death is not at all about closure, but about opening.

Love never dies, honey. In fact, it gets stronger and bolder and deeper when we acknowledge the reality of what's beyond, when we learn to listen with bigger ears.

Mom had very big ears.

So these pages carry both of our voices, allowing room for yours as well. Sometimes I'm not sure if it's Mom's voice or mine, or even yours, coming through. Because we are all One in this circle of creative expression... inspired by the bluebird perched on my shoulder.

"Zip-a-dee-doo-dah, zip-a-dee-ay
My, oh my, what a wonderful day..."

Keep singing your favorite song, Mom. We can hear you.

•••

*For Mom and me, Spirit, One, and God all refer to Divinity...within and beyond us. In our view, Divinity is *absolute* Love, Light, Truth, and Life— as opposed to *personal* love, light, truth, and life. Throughout our dialogues, when these words vibrate with the poetry of Divinity, they are capitalized.

—

Introduction

...

Allow for the space, honey, not just the words.

Mom never wrote anything that didn't contain at least one ellipsis. The three dots were a metaphor for the way she lived Life—opening to its mystery while inviting others into its questions.

So one day, in meditation, I held the symbol of the ellipsis and Mom's unwavering appeal (through mediums, dreams, astrologers, runes...) to *write this thing*. After a brief sit, I grew frustrated.

What thing, Mom? What is it? Give me a genre. Give me some structure. I like structure. Give me something, please.

And she led me to her journals. A reflection of her attention-deficit laced multitudes, her inner and outer worlds, and her unyielding zest for Life. Filled with to-do lists, phone numbers, blessings, sacred numbers, mantras, questions, messages from her guides, house plans, heartworm pill schedules, appointment reminders, declarations of gratitude, recipes, skin care regimens, rough drafts, rituals, intentions, health tips, travel plans, and love. Undeniable Love.

Like a good writer-researcher-control freak, I took copious notes on her meanderings and what I knew of the feelings and experiences behind them. Then I spent hours wading through the randomness, trying to make sense of the project before me.

Overwhelmed, I retreated to the shower, always a place of renewal and baptism. A place where it feels safe to leave the mind and enter the heart. In the steamy echo of this space, I asked, or rather demanded,

"What does it want to be, Mom?"

And I had to jump out of the shower to capture her words on paper.

It wants to be everything, honey. It's one big ELLIPSIS...

...an endless series of breaths, leading from one memory, one mystery, to the next—an organic flow of Life across lifetimes. It's you writing your blood and your tears and your laughter, with me on your shoulder.

But what's the common theme, Mom, the thread that weaves it all together?

It's me, Nicki Beans. And you. And everyone who chooses to join our circle. It's us making magic and meaning together across the realms of reality. It's about the questions that unite us all. It's about telling the truth, as we perceive it, in a moment of imperfect recollection. It's about getting naked with Life. Honoring the stories behind the stories, the pain and longing underneath the beauty and bliss.

It's about the karmic history with which we came into this incarnation, the genetic patterns of our ancestral line, and our individual psychological blueprints. It's about shining Light on all of it...healing it...and then awakening from the dream of it.

You don't need a plan, honey. Just begin the journey—one step, one page at a time. This is new landscape. Let's explore it together—you and me...and we.

A poem landed on my heart, in your voice...

Remember...
Those blades once held wings.
The ache is sweet memory.
Rebirth your wings,
Break through the density of duality,
Fly...

•••

Oh Mama, your faith in the wilderness of this project is admirable. And I am ready to fly with you. But I think you can appreciate my need for rhythm, for cycles, for a little structure. So let's write this in a way that allows me some direction over how these pages unfold. I'm still in human form, remember. I need a little control here.

Control is an illusion, Nicki Beans.

So we'll allow the natural world to lead us in this sacred dance.

I love to dance!

The seasons will be our partners, each one playing the music of a dominant element. Of course, there will be lots of overlaps. Straight lines are a function of mathematics, not of dancing—and certainly not of Life.

No straight lines. That's good, honey.

Winter corresponds to the time we can most easily dip into our deepest waters, reflecting on the lake of our souls, the ocean of our hearts. It is a time of stillness and pondering.

It's a time to hibernate and do our inner work. Remember those silver charms I bought for you and your sister? They said, "Wild rivers run deep in hearts full of love."

I love the depth of a watery winter, bearing witness to the rivers that run through me.

Winter is your season, honey. Its resonance will linger through the seasons of our story.

From winter, we open the doors to the fresh air of spring. The season of birth and growth, ideas and action. As we build our lives, we acknowledge the power of our breath. We expand and blossom.

Spring also holds intoxicating beauty. Don't forget to honor the beauty, Nicki Beans.

Never, Mom. Not with you on my shoulder.

And then summer arrives like wildfire. We are passionate, blazing with the full manifestation of our Divine essence. We are unstoppable as we learn and burn.

Your sister, Holly, is the fire of summer. She is a force of nature.

So is my husband, Mike. Did I marry my sister?

Lots of steam created upon the meeting of your water and their fire, honey. The most valuable learning occurs in the collision of opposites.

And when we grow weary of the friction, when we are ready to lay it all down, we fall into your season...

...and return to the earth. We shift our perspectives, shed our egos, and remember our Truth. In autumn, we are a chaos of random color. We are luminous.

You can see the Light and color in everyone, Mom. It's one of your many gifts.

I like this, Nicki Beans. And the perfect symbol for our natural evolution through these pages is Oakley.

Your tree.

Well, I am more his than he is mine.

It was Oakley's spirit that brought you to Idlywood, his home for over three hundred years and your last home on Earth.

There is nothing more beautiful than an old oak tree, rooted in ancient wisdom and reaching toward Heaven. Yes... Oakley will guide us through this spiral of Life and awakening. He is our mirror, our medicine, and our muse...

•••

WINTER

...

I took the day off, Mom. I am in your office behind my computer. A candle has been lit. It's been fifty days since you passed and there's a new moon today. The creative cycle in my astrological chart is closing this week and I'm not sure when it will reopen. We just entered the year of the Monkey in the Chinese zodiac... I am definitely feeling that manic monkey energy! Now is the time to begin this wild co-creation with you, to get busy with this crazy idea with which we have made a contract. Let's get er' done, as Grandpa would say.

Man, I think I had too much coffee this morning! I'm so ready, Mom. Let's write…

(Silence)

Mom? You there?

(More silence)

Finally, I hear you sigh.

Patience, Nicki. Look out the window. Can you see Oakley? How still he is? Be the tree, Nicki. The first step in the manifestation of any vision, honey, is to intentionally take no step at all.

From the window, I can see the winter trees, so raw and vulnerable. I crack the window so that I might hear their silent conversations. Oakley whispers to me like a great grandfather. This is what he says:

"Plant your feet in the earth, my child. Intermingle your roots with ours. Extend your bare branches and give thanks for this season of peace, this time to hibernate in the cave of your innate wisdom. Humans like to think of winter as the end, when in fact it is the beginning. Rest now in the nature of you."

Dear Oakley, that is all really beautiful in theory, but I'm not tired! And for my own human sanity, I need to get something done today.

Nicki, Nicki, Nicki. This is not something to get done. This is the heart aching and opening to creativity and connection in a way the mind cannot comprehend. Grasping for accomplishment will not lessen your pain. Everything that really matters, everything that will ultimately help you feel whole again, is in the process. And this part of the process is not in the doing, but in the being.

Ugh. I like to check things off my list.

Lie down, honey. Close your big brown eyes and rest your pretty little head. Listen to the trees. They were here long before you were born, and they will be here long after you are gone. They know.

•••

Winter is magical. The earth is pregnant with possibility and I am pregnant with you, Mom. Sometimes I don't know where you end and where I begin. I can feel your blood pulsing through the chambers of my heart, and I can hear your laughter in mine. I am intoxicated by the scent of your lotions on my skin. I am drunk on you. I stare at your ring on my finger and see your hand, a landscape of veins through which our wild rivers run. What shall we do with our hands today?

I walk in your boots, fast and furious, so purpose filled. Things to do. Places to go. But I am heavy with the weight of two souls in one form. Whose eyes are drinking in the world, Mom?

How can I feel so full of you and so empty? Can you hear me, Mom?

I hear you, honey. Breathe. I am in your surrender...

•••

I need to go back to the deep winter of your life, Mom, to your last months on Earth. I need to get it all on paper.

There was a lot of sadness in that time, honey. But there was also immeasurable Love. Let's remember together.

For your family, the winter began in July. But you had been enduring the chill for much longer. Two years, almost to the day of your death, Holly and I were with you in the hospital room after your first biopsy. We heard your gynecologist say, "small stripe on the uterus... precancerous...need to operate." But your voice was louder.

No hospitals. No surgery. I will do this my way.

And we listened. Because your intuition was stronger than any doctor's opinion.

It was a conscious choice, not only for me, but also for you girls. I needed you to see me in my truth, no matter the consequences...

We saw you Mom. And we walked with you on your path. We acknowledged the infection in your uterus. We witnessed your escalating pain.

Everywhere I went, I carried my hot water bottle with me. The warmth provided temporary relief, but the aching in my abdomen was relentless. I was never still, always pacing, trying to move the monster in my belly...

We introduced you to marijuana.

Mike and Holly were master teachers, but smoking didn't feel natural to me. I tried the gummy bears, but they made me feel funny too. Anyway, grandmas don't do dope.

So we stuck to your path, Mom. We believed, because you did, that acupuncture, herbal supplements, and energy work would ultimately revitalize the unhealthy cells in your uterus and bring balance back to your system.

We never called it cancer.

On my healing journey, there was no reason to call it cancer. Cancer is just an infection. To cure it, our cells need to be reminded of their proper function. Cancer creates fear and weakness. It was not a word for me...

You were so much more than this disease. You would not allow yourself to be defined by it.

People mean well, but they love to talk. They want to share their experiences, their opinions, their advice. Everyone has a cancer story. But I had a different perspective, and I didn't have the energy to defend it. I devoted all of my energy to my healing.

As your pain increased, Holly and I took turns accompanying you to your weekly acupuncture appointments. We listened to your healer and took detailed notes, while you endured the penetrating impact of needle after needle. You showed no fear in your steadfast determination to heal your whole self.

This journey was about much more than easing my pain, masking my symptoms. It was about reconciling generations of repressed emotions and deep wounds, bringing the pain to the surface to be seen and released...so that you girls wouldn't have to carry it.

You were healing all of us, your ancestors and your descendants.

My body—my blood, my breath, my organs—told stories that weren't mine. Some were, but not all. In many ways, my pain was universal. It belonged to humanity.

And you allowed it to manifest in you. So that it could transform through you.

Spirit gave me the strength to embody this pain. For all of us. It was a Divine deal made in no-time. I would transform this torment into Truth...in exchange for two angels as daughters.

Thank you, Mom.

You're welcome, honey.

•••

After a year of intense acupuncture, your healer said it was time to see a surgeon. The needles, the herbs, and your body's wisdom had worked together to form a singular mass of disease that was ready to be removed. Metaphorically, all the dirt in your house had been swept into one neat pile. All that was needed now was the surgeon's dustpan.

If only it could have been that simple.

The road into western medicine was paved with questions and scans and blood tests and language that was at once foreign and familiar. Our family doctor delivered the news to me. News that wasn't really news.

"Cancer," he said.
"Cancer," I repeated back to him.
"Cancer," I would have to say out loud to you and Dad and Holly and Mike and the kids.

I'm so sorry you had to carry the weight of that word by yourself.

Only for a few moments, Mom. As soon as I got in the car, I called Mike…and allowed the dam to break. The dam I'd unconsciously built to keep that word from my awareness. With one violent exhale, the river holding that word broke loose. In its rush, my husband did not falter. He absorbed me in his silence as I sat parked on the side of the road, my wailing drowned out by the flow of passing traffic.

With every surge of tears, Mike kept you afloat. Riding the waves of that word with you. Until they settled…and you were ready to come back to Idylwood, back to me.

When I walked into the house, you were sitting at the kitchen table talking on the phone. You were smiling, your eyebrows raised, as you watched me get a glass of water. The air was saturated with the aroma of grilled cheese and tomato soup. Our comfort food. I wanted to swim in the soup and use the grilled cheese as a raft. I longed to immerse myself in your maternal nurturing…to return to childhood, to innocence, to life before that word.

You hung up the phone and I sat down beside you, unable to meet your eyes. You said the word out loud—so I didn't have to.

Cancer.

All those months of not ever speaking it…and all of a sudden, it was the only word on my lips. It was begging to be spoken. It wanted to be set free.

Cancer joined us for our lunch of comfort food…and it never left. For the week leading up to your appointment with the surgeon, we did our best to adjust to its dark presence. It corrupted every step, every breath we took. But there was still hope. The surgeon and her dustpan would surely take away your pain…and ours.

There was hope.

Remember walking the labyrinth, Mom?

It was just the four of us, our little nuclear family. And the dogs underfoot. You all wore such sad faces and I couldn't bear it. I started singing.

"Ain't nothin' gonna break-a my stride, nobody gonna slow me down, oh no, I got to keep on movin'…"

We all joined in, singing your song, touching hands as we passed each other on the weaving path. You made us believe that you would keep on moving, that we would keep on moving.

How could I not heal with the power of your Love surrounding me?

We held hands in the center of the labyrinth. I don't remember the words spoken. They didn't really matter.

Nothing matters but Love, honey.

•••

The four of us got up at the crack of dawn to make the trip to the hospital for your meeting with the surgeon. Driven by our faith in your inevitable recovery, we were like a band of missionaries marching into the cancer center. Certainly, the doctor would recognize the truth of our message. "Yes, your mom is sick," she would say, "and yes, this surgery will save her."

But that's not how it unfolded, was it, honey?

18

It was clear from the moment the intern came in to review your case that our declaration of hope would fall on deaf ears.

With a furrowed brow, he studied the file in front of him and shook his head ever so slightly. When he finally looked up at me, his face was a shadow of judgement. From his western medical perspective, the recovery path I had chosen had no value. By not coming to the hospital sooner, I had written my own death sentence.

Holly and Dad decided that I should be the one to stay with you through the examination. I had become more comfortable with the intimacies of your condition. But the pain you endured, the unyielding blood and tears, was unthinkable. And there was nothing I could do about it. Except hold your hand and whisper, "Almost done…," which was really more of a question for the doctor than reassuring words for you. I was drowning in your pain.

For the first time as your mother, I was too consumed by my own suffering to support you in yours. With this agonizing awareness, I began to doubt myself and my choices. This doubt opened the door for fear. And in my fragile state of mind, fear stormed in.

After the exam, we were led to a "family room" that was designed to provide comfort for patients and their loved ones. It didn't. Under the unforgiving, fluorescent lights, we all sat together to hear the doctor's horrible words, "too advanced…inoperable…a few months at best."

It was shocking, yet somehow expected.

And we just accepted it. How could we have so quickly raised our white flag of surrender? You, the champion of intuition, and we, the disciples of your word—all folding under the opinion of one doctor, one HUMAN doctor. If only we had taken a moment to turn off the blinding lights and sit in our collective silence, in our truth…we would have remembered.

The power of the white coat is hypnotic. The doctor's interpretation of my condition, her version of truth, seemed indisputable.

All we could do was cry and hold each other as the parade of white coats came through the room to share their insights, their experiences with other patients and families, their desire to help us on this leg of the journey. A standard protocol of support, like a cast for our broken hearts.

They sent us for another scan. Did they need more proof of my demise? No one had the energy to question their directives. As a family, we lumbered through the cancer wing of the hospital. In the waiting area, there were people who were yellow with disease. I could not meet anyone's gaze. I had no smile to offer. I felt like a child, awakening to a nightmare. I just wanted to close my eyes.

We got coffee and peanut butter crackers and found a seat on the vinyl bench the color of vomit. It was crowded and the optimistic scent of soap hung in the air, as if it might clean the illness from the room. I went outside to call Mike. The summer heat was suffocating.

"It's bad," I told him. "I'm coming," he said.

I sobbed on the sidewalk, hanging on to a railing meant for disabled people. In that moment, I was disabled. A passerby with gentle eyes stopped to embrace me. No words were spoken. In the holy hush of a stranger's hug, I found the strength to go back inside the hope-sucking hospital, back to the vomit-colored bench, back to you.

After the x-ray, I just wanted to go home. But they said I had another test... in another building. I was so tired.

You needed an ultrasound to check for blood clots. In the car, you pulled out your makeup bag.

Despair is no excuse to let yourself go, honey. At the time, it felt like the only thing I could control.

You put eyeliner on your lips, Mom.

Maybe I did that on purpose—to make you laugh. Or maybe I wanted to be goth.

You and I went in for the ultrasound appointment. Dad and Holly went to get lunch for us...although all you wanted was potato chips.

Never a time when a chip didn't hit the spot.

Holly said your song was playing at the sandwich shop.

"Ain't nothin' gonna break-a my stride, nobody gonna slow me down..."

Yep. It was a sign. We were going to be alright. Somehow. We would keep on movin'…

Then Mike came. With a single tear rolling down his cheek, he knelt down to hug me. I whispered in his ear, "I knew, I knew." Like it was a secret only he could keep.

You are his mom too.

He is the son I never had.

Your ultrasound brought more bad news.

Clots. Which called for more western medicine, more chemicals going into my body, on top of the narcotics prescribed by the surgeon. All the work I'd done to clear my system of toxins and disease, to make myself whole again, was being wiped out in a single day.

Broken, we drove home. Mike was already there heating up an array of colorful and savory leftovers. The sights and scents of the kitchen brought familiar comfort, but no one was hungry. You found solace on the couch with your dogs.

Happy jumped up on the sofa beside me and Selma curled up at my feet. Their warmth took the chill from my bones, for a moment. I closed my eyes and slept with my hand on Happy's soft ears. Such sweet contentment.

And I got busy, which is what I do in the midst of hardship. I wrote an email to your friends, those who were planning on being with you the following month for your fiftieth wedding anniversary party. I asked for their prayers.

> Dearest friends of Nancy and Bill,
>
> As some of you are aware, we will be postponing the anniversary celebration. Mom has been fighting illness for a year now. The doctors are calling it the C word. A rare form. Like mom. Not as responsive to treatment. Likely inoperable. **We ask that you all light a candle at seven o'clock, beginning tonight and for the next three nights…and hold Mom in the Light**. The power of collective prayer is transforming. We need your Love and Light.

While the doctors are using the C word, please know and honor that we are visualizing this as a rebirth for mom. She was chosen to carry this pain because of her strength and ability to transform universal pain into Love. Now she is in labor and needs our help, OUR LOVE, to deliver this pain once and for all. Ultimately, this experience will serve as wisdom to guide Mom as she teaches and inspires others—the work she's always done and is meant to continue doing. Please hold Mom in the image of Love and vibrancy—NO FEAR! We can heal her with our LOVE so that she can rebirth herself into Life.

Wow. We do know how to emit some optimism, don't we, baby girl?

We learned that from Grandma. "Just smile and be nice and it will all be just fine."

It's good advice, until it isn't. And you have to face the shadow...

I wasn't ready to face it yet, Mom. Not completely. A part of me needed to believe that we could smile and be nice and it would all be just fine. I needed to rest in Grandma's mantra, for a little while.

On the first of those three nights, we all sat together in the den, in the comfort of knowing that many others were sharing this moment with us. Such a solemn scene, accented by the rhythm of the rain and the beating of our hearts. There was no room for words.

The rain started that evening and continued for nearly a week. It seemed that Mother Nature had alchemized the weather just for us, a reflection of our emotion, a reminder to release.

The next day, we all gathered on the screened porch. It was quite literally a perfect storm. The thunder, the lightning, the pounding rain...

...and a phone call from the surgeon informing us that, after speaking with our family doctor, she might consider surgery after all. It was a ray of sunlight through our perfect storm.

As a family, we talked over the deafening downpour. It had become clear to me that surgery was not the answer. My body was too weak to tolerate any kind of major invasion. I would not die in a hospital. I would live my last days at Idylwood, in the serenity provided by pain pills...and Love.

The thunder cued my rage.

You let it all out, honey.

The lightning was an electrifying jolt into a future without you. The rain had nothing on my tears.

I thought you were going to throw up. I told your sister to get you a bucket.

You made me laugh, Mom. For a moment, I could see beyond my pain to the calm in your eyes. You were at peace with the choices you had made.

There was peace, along with a gnawing exhaustion. I just wanted to sleep.

After this family dialogue that left us all wrecked and weary, I went to the outdoor shower. It was a baptism, the shower mixed with my tears and the rain. I howled at Spirit until I was completely empty. And surrendered. There is a sign in the shower that reads, "Love Like a Golden," and it made me smile. Golden retriever love is Divine Love, absolute and pure. It would guide us on this new path, the path to death. We would be with you every step of the way, Mom.

•••

Western medicine was the answer to your prayer for deep, uninterrupted sleep.

It was, but I hated the side effects—the confusion, the loss of body control, the nausea. It was all so indelicate.

Yet you found the silver lining of most every cloud that crossed your sky. You'd look in the mirror and say, "I still have great hair."

Did I? Well, it was true. True all the way to the end. I had great hair. Hair is power, honey. Never forget that.

Up until the week before you passed, one of the first questions you'd ask every morning was, "Do I have a hair appointment today?" I would just roll my eyes and shake my head. I wanted you to use your limited energy for excursions that would make you feel better, like an appointment at the float tank or a session with the reiki therapist.

And for me, getting my hair done did make me feel better. It was my last connection to the life I knew and loved. Being in a salon, with the doting stylists and all the pretty products, made me forget that I was sick, for a little while.

Your beauty routine was your lifeline. I would tuck you in at night and you'd say, "Oh, wait, just one more thing…," and you'd shuffle into the bathroom to get a serum for your face, a cream for your hands or feet.

In the morning, I'd ask Spirit to help me with my contacts or my makeup. It was less about vanity and more an effort to hold on to the rituals that defined my days.

You'd get frustrated when I tried to help. "Stop asking me so many questions. Just let me do it," you'd say.

The contacts were the worst. Often I couldn't remember if I'd put them in or not, but even when my mind was clear, my hands were too unsteady to complete the task. I felt completely defeated when I had to start wearing glasses.

You hated your new glasses.

I wanted to like what I saw when I looked in the mirror. That was vanity, I suppose. Beauty was a big part of my identity. The thought of losing it caused me great suffering.

And as your journey progressed, you gained a profound appreciation for your inner beauty, Mom. About anything external—smudged makeup or a dirty shirt—you would say, with your hand resting on your heart, "It doesn't matter."

That time was such a blur. It was as if I had one foot in Heaven and one foot here on Earth. When I was alert, I could see things that you couldn't.

Like the people walking through the family room, the white horses on the lawn, the faces on the trees, the giraffe in the bathtub, the rabbit on the bicycle, the cat on Dad's shoulder...

"Get that cat off his shoulder," you told Mike...and my sweet husband shewed the cat off Dad's shoulder.

I was doing and saying some strange things...seeing beyond this reality and falling into my truth—and the Truth. I sang when I wanted to sing, screamed when I wanted to scream, and cried when I wanted to cry. There is freedom that comes with dying.

One of my most treasured memories from that time occurred on the screened porch...on a perfect summer day. An easy breeze invited the wind chimes to harmonize with the sweet songs of the birds and the gentle cascade of the fountain. We basked in the warmth of the day, soothed by the scent of lavender in the air and entertained by the squirrels chasing each other through the canopy of trees.

I remember. Mike and the kids were there—Grace and Viv at my feet and Rhode snuggled up close to me. Holly's Dave blew in with a bouquet of roses. They were white, my favorite color.

Randy, our priest and friend, was there too. With a soft grin on his face, he was drinking in all the Love surrounding you when he said,

"This is the best stuff of Life."

Yes. This is the best stuff of Life. And we all sang a song that had become your new favorite. A song that you roared from the deepest part of you. A song that felt like a joyful prayer, a calling out to Life...

"Zip-a-dee-doo-dah, zip-a-dee-ay
My, oh my, what a wonderful day
Plenty of sunshine headin' my way
Zip-a-dee-doo-dah, zip-a-dee-ay..."

•••

On the night of the Aquarius full moon, I had lucid dreams. In one, I was you—in your body, feeling your pain. In another, I was a little girl. And you were tucking me into bed, stroking my hair, whispering words of reassurance...just as I had tucked you in hours before. I woke to a bath of moonlight and a wailing release of grief over my loss of you. But with this release came gratitude upon knowing that you would never leave me. I would always find you in my dreams.

Always.

The next day, we received a gift.

Dr. Zach Bush...

...our family doctor and our knight shining without armor...a pure embodiment of Truth. He came to rescue us from our hopelessness.

Dr. Bush had seen me through my illness, offering candid opinions on my condition and various options to explore, yet always respecting the paths I chose.

He awakened us that day, to what we had forgotten in our fear. You had a choice, Mom. You could live, or you could die. It was up to you.

This brilliant and dear man opened my eyes to my right to claim this life.

By the end of his visit, we were all screaming,

"I AM NANCY!"

With every declaration of self, I celebrated my identity and my boundaries, my will to stay in this form. My body was vibrating with power! My cells were alight with joy!

Dr. Bush told us that cancer was simply a signal that you had yet to become your truest self. There was still more of you to discover. Cancer was giving you the opportunity to explore and reclaim your authority to be here and now.

And thus began the regimen of of what the doc called "communication tools" that would remind my body of its proper functions. These tools would serve to reconnect me to life...and to Life.

Holly made a sign that said, "I AM NANCY." She filled in each bubble letter with the boldest colors she could find. The crayons were mere nubs by the time she finished with them. That sign traveled with you from room to room so you would never forget your intention to heal.

Yes...and at times, that was a heavy sign to carry from room to room, day after day. As much as I wanted to maintain my original enthusiasm for this rally, I was still so tired. You and your sister were a mighty force behind the new healing agenda, always delivering liquids for me to drink from my beautiful pottery engraved with messages like, "cup of love," "cup of gratitude," "cup of a new day." So precious, yet the simple act of swallowing was such an effort. Your anticipation and expectations were exhausting.

Your hospice team could see that Holly and I needed a shift in perspective. These wise women were able to express to us what you wouldn't say. Their words widened our lens on Love.

It was necessary, honey. We were merged in a way that made it hard for you to see ME through your hope. My love for you and your sister and your dad was monumental...but I had to love Nancy more.

So we learned to listen more deeply, to discern when we needed to push and when we needed to let you rest. We put our agenda aside so that we could just be with you in the Truth of each moment.

And in that surrender, you allowed me the space to heal—in my own time.

As you slept, we sat beside your bed. We placed our hands on the tumor that seemed to expand and contract, harden and soften with your breath. It had a life force of its own. Instead of railing against it, we sent it loving energy through our silent prayers and tears...willing it to release its hold on you.

I could feel you there. Our sacred and still time together was the best medicine of all.

I remember a morning on the front porch. After three days of rain, the sun finally emerged from the clouds.

Those rays were a gift from Heaven. Lying on the chaise lounge, smiling up at the Light.

You were luminous, Mom. I was at your feet, massaging your tender toes. "Please, God," I chanted over and over. We fell into a deep meditation, sharing a holy space beyond this dimension. After what seemed like hours, you opened your eyes and said, "Where *were* we?"

And you said, "With God."

I meant it, Mom. Spirit shed sweet grace on us that day.

Thank you, Spirit. Thank you, thank you, thank you...

•••

The next weeks brought ever-changing tides. There were times when you were barely coherent...and times when you roared with your intention to live, demanding a pen and paper to make a list.

I could hardly write, but it seemed vitally important to record my thoughts—friends I wanted to call, supplements I needed to take, grocery items I had to have. I would not allow us to run out of potato chips.

I loved those days, Mom...when your old temper flared as you took back your life. You'd tell us we were all crazy and nudge us out of the way so that you could make yourself a cup of coffee, the way you wanted it.

As much as I appreciated the care you and your sister provided, sometimes I just wanted to be alone in my kitchen, making my own coffee or eating as many chips as I pleased. On the rare days that Spirit granted me some strength, I used it to assert my will. And it felt good.

We reveled in your feisty outbursts, Mom. Your anger would, no doubt, motivate the transformation of this disease. From the top of your lungs, you'd scream, "I AM NANCY!"

I shook the house with my power!

You shook the Earth with your power.

Until the exhaustion returned.

There was Truth in your rage and in your retreat, Mom. Holly and I wanted to be there for all of it. Just like you'd been there for us...

Like we've been there for each other...across lifetimes.

Beside your "I AM NANCY" sign, we placed a portrait of you as a baby. Sometimes when we'd try to impose a plan on you—eating or bathing or moving—you'd say, or rather sigh, your mouth turned up in a gentle grin, "Oh, not now, let me just sit and stare at me for a while." And so we'd sit and stare...at the brilliance of you.

I learned to love myself wholeheartedly on those days of what might have seemed like total resignation from life. I was shining my most authentic Light, my acceptance of whatever each moment delivered.

I fed you chicken soup in the bathtub on an evening that pulsed with peace. To me, you had never felt more real or looked more beautiful. When I told you as much, you didn't dismiss me. You agreed. You knew how radiant you were, not in spite of your illness, but because of it. You had been cracked wide open and what emerged was a sincerity beyond pride, beyond ego, beyond words.

I'm so grateful that we had those moments. And that you have those memories.

•••

One morning, we all went to see Dr. Bush, our family doctor in the truest sense of the term. Dad drove, and Holly and I held hands in the back seat. It was a quiet ride. No music. No idle chatter. You broke the silence with a message, laced with regret, "Life can be hard, girls. I think I forgot to tell you that part."

I did forget to tell you that part. For me, being a good mother sometimes meant putting on a happy face when I wasn't really happy. When things were hard. Rose-colored glasses are lovely, until they stop working. And they always stop working.

After your appointment, we drove to a campground overlooking the river. We took off your shoes so you could feel the earth on your soles and in your soul.

The air smelled blissfully fresh. Like honeysuckle. Maybe the air by the river is always so fragrant. I just hadn't noticed before...

It was a bittersweet afternoon. So simple, just watching the mighty James race over and around the rocks, as we munched on the Fritos we'd bought at the camp store. Dad loves Fritos. And the water lightens him, reminds him to exhale and flow, even in the rapids. We threw Fritos at each other...and we laughed. Our laughter opened us to joy.

Without our rose-colored glasses, the joy of us was even clearer.

Bare feet, family, and Fritos. The best stuff of Life.

•••

Confusion was a constant companion in my final season.

We tried to find humor in some of your strange comments, for your sake and ours. You once confused a maxi pad liner for a receipt. Handing it to me, you said, "You hold on to that, Nicki Beans. I need to reimburse you."

Oh dear. That is funny.

But within an hour of a delusional remark, you would say something so wise and random like, "Being present requires some silence. Let's just be silent now, honey."

A moment of clarity was a rare gift of Light...and I didn't want to overshadow it with the weight of wearisome words.

On your fiftieth wedding anniversary, the monster in your belly raged. But you rallied for Dad and the whole family. Your words, while weary, were so very sweet. We hung on every one.

You and Holly prepared a delightful dinner—crab cakes and baked potatoes by candlelight. Grace, who had just started her first job at a bakery, made us a layered lemon cake. She knew how much I loved lemons. I forced myself to eat a few bites of this love-filled meal, to show you all my gratitude. Your dad looked sad—his eyes grayer than blue on this golden anniversary. I hoped he could see my love for him shining through this family, through this life we had designed and built together.

You two had brilliant vision.

We were not a couple that snuggled and stared wistfully into one another's eyes. Our love was in our movement...holding hands and walking toward the next horizon. Together. Always together.

We played your wedding song, "Summer's Place," and you said, "Oh, I know this one, it's 'Farmer's Night.'"

You all laughed, while Dad and I danced our final dance. I was wearing my bathrobe, but it didn't matter. Dad looked at me as if I were the most beautiful bride in the world. After feeding me a bite of lemon wedding cake, he danced me back to bed, where I would sleep for most of the next few weeks.

We worried incessantly. Would you ever wake up?

I was on the other side of a magical mirror during that time. I got quite a view of my life.

Energetically, you stayed connected to all of us, including your grandchildren. Grace felt you most acutely. In her visceral despair, she questioned Mike daily, "What will we do without Nonie?"

I heard her. From behind the mirror, somehow I could see and hear all of you. I watched your children rising to care for themselves while you were caring for me. I watched your sister twirling and drumming at a music festival, a recess for her soul. I watched your husband in his topless Jeep, screaming at the sky on his way up Route 6.

He would drive to Idlywood after work and on the weekends. I'd meet him at the back gate—his face tear-stained, his voice rough.

I saw it all, honey.

And you decided to stay…

Yes. I knew how much my family wanted and needed me, but that was secondary to the Life I still had left to live for Nancy. I fell in Love with me behind that magical mirror. And I chose to wake up from my long summer's nap, to remain Earthbound...for a little longer.

We were all outside by Oakley when we heard you calling from your bedroom. We raced inside to find you bright-eyed and bewildered. "Did I die?" you asked, with the innocence of a little girl. We were speechless. *Had* part of you died behind that mirror? Who was this beautiful child before us? And what mysteries did she have to share?

The only mystery that interested me at the time was what was for lunch. I woke up with a hunger I'd never experienced before, like I was a teenage boy! I couldn't get enough. It was as if food was Life...and I was eager to savor it!

In awe, we watched you devour every feast we put before you. The more carbs and calories, the better. Sometimes you'd finish a meal with more food on your shirt than in your belly. Holly and I would suggest you change your clothes, and you'd tell us…

It doesn't matter. Can I have a few more chips?

Everything you ate was the "best ever."

This is the best tomato soup ever. This is the best pasta ever. This is the best cheese puff ever.

You'd get hungry in the middle of the night, so we'd leave a bowl of cheese puffs on your bedside table.

Those would be gone by midnight.

Once, I came downstairs to find you and dad eating chocolate pudding and potato chips at three o'clock in the morning. Dad was in his underwear, and you two were giggling like little children. With my hands on my hips, I stood there shaking my head and laughing at the absurdity of this poignant role reversal, this precious scene.

Your dad and I fell in love all over again in that scene…over pudding and potato chips!

And then it was your birthday.

And Grace's birthday…so we had to go shopping, of course.

Of course. We drove into town to check out your favorite store. You wanted to get something for Viv too.

Well, sure, my Vivi had to have something too. But first, we had to get some noodles at Noodles & Company.

Right. How could I forget the noodles? You ate them in the car while I went into the store.

I was hungry! But I sent you in with a very specific vision of what I wanted for the girls. I always knew the trends, even before the fashion industry announced them.

And, like always, your vision was manifested. It's like you have a connection with the fashion goddesses.

I am a fashion goddess, honey. And on that day, I worked through you to find the hippest fall sweaters for my granddaughters. The saleslady let you model a few selections for me on the sidewalk, where I could see you from the car.

With noodles on your chin, you gave me your thumb up or down. When I tried to tell you the price of what you liked, you said,

It doesn't matter...

That was a fun day, Mom.

The best ever.

The birthday celebration was pretty great too.

We celebrated big. The whole family came. I felt like a queen on a throne with everyone gathered around me, bringing me more cheese puffs whenever I asked. I wore a flowy, blue dress with a bohemian pattern. It was new.

There was always a new dress or four in your closet, Mom.

You never know when an occasion for a new dress might present itself. A girl has to be ready. And I was ready to celebrate my birthday. That dress was a reflection of the flower child in me. The child who was ready to skip through the daisies again. I just had to get my legs back.

While your spirit was ready to skip, the blood clots in your legs kept you perched on your throne, basking in the September sun, your grandchildren kneeling beside you.

My grandbabies looked at me like I was a miracle.

You are a miracle, Mom.

•••

My birthday was just the start of this new chapter. I wanted the celebration to continue...with a Gratitude Gathering.

We decided to bring all of your friends together, in honor of Life. We sent this:

> Dear Friends,
> You are invited to an open house of open hearts, an expression of my love and gratitude for all your thoughts, prayers, and healing energy. You brought me back! Let's come together for a simple celebration of LIFE... I AM NANCY!

On the day of the gathering, in an unfortunate twist of fate, the familiar ache in my abdomen returned. As I combed my hair and put on my lipstick, I wondered how I would hold both the pain and the party...and the fear that this burden was here to stay.

Spirit helped, Mom. Reminding you that whatever you brought to the gathering was more than enough. And whatever the future held was out of your control. With this awareness, you rose to embrace your moment. People came in flocks to marvel at the wonder of you!

I sat by the fire pit, enlightened by the blaze, allowing Life to unfold within and around me. You and your sister had strung the hundreds of cards and love notes sent by friends over the season and hung them like streamers from the tent. A testament to the Love that brought me back, the Love now present in my backyard.

Throughout the afternoon, we threw those notes and cards into the fire as an offering to Spirit in Heaven...our gratitude for this exquisite October day on Earth.

There was meat smoking and music playing and a line of friends waiting to see me up close. It was a dream within a dream.

Everyone planted a tulip bulb in your gratitude garden. On their knees, your beloveds dug in the dirt with bare hands. In your honor. In Life's honor.

The earth of my garden and the earth my body were one. I could feel the tulips resting within my form. Would I be here to witness their birth in the spring?

Mom, you were already in full bloom.

By the end of the celebration, the pain had settled deep in my bones. I knew. This would be my last hoorah, a perfect party to bookend my days as a hostess.

As a parting gift, everyone took a bulb home to plant in their own gardens. You see, Mom, your days as hostess continue. Every year, those tulips, imbued with your vibrant smile, emerge to welcome us to spring, to nature's most spectacular party...

I like that, Nicki Beans... a tender reminder of everlasting Life.

•••

Over the next fifty days, your physical decline was steady. You became deeply depressed...

...and confused. "Do I live here? Are these my things?" I would ask, floating in between worlds with no anchor. Living in pain and fear is no way to live.

Yet Holly and I kept pushing the supplements and the positive affirmations. And Dad continued chanting his mantra, "Keep fighting, Nance, keep fighting!"

There was a bitterness brewing within me, a resentment of your relentless effort to save me. With my last bit of energy, I raised the white flag, but you refused to see it.

We were blinded by hope, Mom. You had bounced back once before. Certainly, you could do it again.

Thanksgiving came. My favorite day of the year. I woke to the familiar aroma of turkey roasting in the oven. How did it get there? I shuffled into the kitchen to find you and your sister orchestrating my holiday, my show.

You looked right through us, Mom. You couldn't see that the beauty of this Thanksgiving scene was your beauty. Your hands peeling the potatoes. Your tears falling on the onions. Your lips testing the sweetness of the corn pudding.

I was overwhelmed by loss and longing for what was. A potent rage rose within me. It besieged my heart and overpowered Love.

But only for a moment, Mom. Through you, Love had invited Randy for dinner. You didn't want anyone to be alone on this holiday. When he arrived, you softened.

The secret is in the softening, in the surrender. That's how Love wins, honey.

We dined on the porch, the setting of our most memorable family affairs. There was a chill in the air, but the space heaters created a coziness, a warm invitation to gather there with the autumn trees just on the other side of the screen. You sat at the head of the table, taking small and inconsequential bites from the overflowing plate we put before you. We tried to engage you in conversation, but you just stared at the sun fading slowly behind the hill.

I wanted to melt into that sunset, to fade away with the day.

After dinner, in an attempt to lure you back to us, we sang songs around the fire. Dave led us in some folk classics, a few family favorites, and an encore of "Zip-a-Dee-Doo-Dah …"

The music was renewing. I watched Dave's fingers strum the guitar and I listened to your joyful sounds. I held Grace's hand and for a few minutes, I felt happy.

But the next day, you didn't want to get out of bed. So we called Dr. Bush, our guide on your path back to Nancy. Surely, he would have an answer.

He is a good man. So faithful. He couldn't see my white flag either. He said he wanted to dance with me on some island off the coast of Spain. I allowed myself to bask in the glimmer of that possibility, for his sake and yours.

His ray of Light roused you from your bed that day. We convinced you to take a short walk with us to visit Oakley…the king of trees, the king of wisdom and strength.

Every step hurt, but Oakley was calling me. I had to lay my hands on him one last time. For both of us. I asked him to share his medicine with my family and me. I could feel his energy coursing through my veins.

We were all empowered by his majesty...

...for a moment.

The next day, I announced that I was taking you on a road trip to the beach. If we could make it to the tree together, we could make it to the water...together.

It was a foolish and fabulous idea.

I had a vision of our toes in the sand, Mom. Nothing was going to stop me from making it happen.

I didn't have the energy to argue.

The journey there was difficult. You stared out the window, lost in your pain and confusion. The further we traveled from the comfort of home, the more I worried that I'd made a terrible mistake.

I wasn't worried. The gift of our destination was well worth the hardship of our journey. Mother Ocean welcomed us to her shore and invited us to lay down the heavy baggage of our hearts... and rest in her rhythm.

In the embrace of her boundless beauty, she synchronized her breath with ours, so that we were One.

Toes in the sand, holding your hand...

Your best friend, Carol, met us there. You two chattered about ordinary things while I lay in the warm November sand, making angels and thanking Spirit for this day.

I felt normal for a little while. Normal is nice.

The tide took our despair and offered us the bliss of now.

And the promise of eternity...

•••

The following week, we took you to the hospital for a blood transfusion. We were optimistic that this lifeline would give you more energy and clarity of mind. I held your hand, and between naps, you stared into my eyes. You didn't need words to speak to my heart.

It was too much. The sparkly Christmas decorations, the perky nurses, all the questions I couldn't answer without your help. Life was going on all around me and I couldn't engage. It was like watching a movie in which I was expected to perform, but couldn't.

When I left the hospital, on my way to the parking lot, I walked by the window of your room. You were looking at me, but also at something beyond me. You raised your hand to wave...a harbinger of your inevitable goodbye.

You are good at reading hearts, honey.

I learned from the best.

The transfusion did little to improve your condition and you began to disconnect from Holly and me. You were consumed by your pain.

Holly brought me to her house for an overnight change of scenery. She borrowed a wheelchair and rolled me through her neighborhood, desperately trying to shift my focus from the aching within to the beauty all around. Yet the sky and the trees and the happy homes were colorless. My world had become black and white.

So she brought you back to her front porch and got out the coloring books and the colored pencils.

If my world was colorless, then she would color it for me. She put a pencil in my hand, but all I could do was watch her add blue to the sky of the page. It was a pretty blue.

I came over with Rhode that evening. You were sitting on Holly's couch, loosely holding a glass of water that was on the verge of spilling. You gazed at the glass, while Holly and Dave decorated the Christmas tree in front of you, reminding you of the significance of each ornament. Your face displayed no recognition of the shiny green ball that hung on your first Christmas tree with Dad. When I came in, you turned your head toward me, but your eyes landed on your only grandson.

Rhode has the face of an angel. He looked at me without expectation, without false hope. He could be present with me in a way you and your sister could not. He sat beside me, and together, we just watched the movie of my life.

In that tender moment, I opened my heart to a hard reality. Your family, which was your *everything*, was not enough to keep you here.

I had reached the point on my journey where my relationships were no longer reciprocal. I had nothing left to give, and I couldn't live without giving, without playing an active part in my movie. I was ready for the curtain, to be that which was beyond Nancy, beyond the screen of identity.

But Holly and I kept telling you to command your space, to reclaim your boundaries, to be here and now with us...for us.

And all I wanted was for you to stop talking, to stop needing me. I had to make you see, really see, that I was dying into the formless state of reality.

My need for *us* was overshadowing my love for you. I'm sorry, Mom.

Never apologize for your truth, honey.

•••

Your level of pain and dementia continued to increase, indicating a rise in your calcium level and the need for yet another blood transfusion. Dad and I took you to your doctor's office where it was confirmed that a trip to the hospital was imperative. We didn't need to take you immediately. We could wait until the next day to avoid a potential overnight stay. It was up to us.

I was so tired.

The thought of another night at home with you in this amount of pain was too much to bear. We had been shuffling through our days in a haze of hope. Nothing mattered but loving you back to health. We spun positivity like yarn...focused and undeterred in our efforts.

A family gift and curse...

We were shining an artificial light on you, on the cancer. And it was blinding. I just wanted to close my eyes, to let someone else see what needed to be seen.

It was time.

Dad and I decided it would be best to take you to the hospital directly from the doctor's office. You didn't argue. Your eyes revealed both resignation and relief.

At home, engulfed by my familiar luxuries and your unwavering optimism, I couldn't fully yield to my pain. But the hospital, the place that triggered all of my fear, would ultimately give me the permission I needed to surrender.

In the emergency room, you gracefully submitted to test after unnecessary test. The answer, we thought, would be found in a lab result or a doctor's report. But it wasn't. The answer, we discovered, was in your hands. We finally let ourselves see the white flag you'd been waving for weeks.

It unraveled in perfect time, honey. It all needed to happen for you to accept the inevitable Truth. Only then could I could lay down the flag and rest in my surrender.

We were in the emergency room for almost twelve hours before a room became available for you. It was in the orthopedic wing, where you would be attended by nurses who were well-meaning but ill-equipped to administer the level of care you required. I cringed as they cocooned your delicate body in a sheet and moved you from the stretcher to the bed. You cried out in anguish, but I couldn't find my voice. "Careful," I whispered, as they talked of mundane things over you, oblivious to your brilliance and the magnitude of the tragedy before them.

I was finally allowing myself to be one with my pain. I didn't have to pretend at the hospital. As difficult as it was to be there, it was also freeing.

The nurses could hardly believe you had only been taking ibuprofen for your pain. When the doctor suggested morphine, we knew it was the end.

I had quite a tolerance for this disease, until I just didn't anymore.

The morphine helped for short periods, but also made you extremely agitated and combative. We would learn later that the dosage wasn't nearly strong enough. You still hurt so much.

My spirit was yearning to leave my body. But my body was a tough little thing. It was hanging on.

•••

I left you when Holly got to the hospital. I needed to drive far away from your suffering...to a place that vibrated with vitality, to the school where I taught second grade. On my way to my classroom, I found Mary, my dear friend and colleague. Under her soft gaze, I made a sound that I didn't recognize as my own, a deep and primitive release of sorrow that I'd been carrying for what seemed like a lifetime. Mary took my hand and led me into the forest. In what felt at once like shocking betrayal and sweet liberation, I let the words I'd been harboring escape from the lump in my throat, "My mom is dying."

Part of me was already gone and with you and Mary in the sacred silence of the woods. Knowing there were no words big enough for this moment, Mary allowed space for the angels to whisper to your heart. Long after she left, her Love lingered...

Sitting on the trunk of a fallen tree, I ran my hand over the moss that continued to thrive there. Its green vibrance was a gentle reminder that Life does indeed continue after death.

A message I sent through the angels...

I laid my body across the tree and let the tender moss dry my tears. Then I left the forest for my classroom, where I was embraced by the arms of eighteen second graders. The arms of Life longing to be lived. I inhaled the beauty and despair of this scene until my lungs were full and my soul could speak my gratitude.

The Love of children is the best elixir for suffering.

Yes, it is. Thank you, little angels...

•••

Holly spent the second night with you in the hospital. Your agitation had increased and she struggled to keep you calm and comfortable. Witnessing your distress was agonizing for her.

Your sister is a warrior. What I might have hidden from you, I could let her see. But I think that dark night in the hospital broke part of her spirit. She continued to fight for me...in a brutal battle she couldn't win.

When I arrived back at the hospital, I found her standing over you, her bright eyes dim. She seemed smaller than the almost six-foot-tall woman I had looked up to all my life, as if a piece of herself, the peace of herself, had retreated with you. I took her hand and we wandered through the halls until our legs grew weak from the weight of our hearts. We collapsed into two plush chairs that didn't seem to belong in a hospital corridor—as if they were waiting to hold us in our time of need. I made Holly promise she wouldn't move. From the chair. From Richmond. I didn't know what I meant. And it didn't matter. She promised. And I knew...my big sister would never leave me. That was all that mattered in the moment. We sat in silence for seconds, minutes, lifetimes... watching the passersby until we found the courage to walk back to your room.

I could hear your muffled voices outside my door. The doctor, the hospice team, you girls and your dad—all busy making plans for my release from the hospital, my release from the world.

We knew you would want to take your last breath at home. The ambulance drivers arrived with gentle eyes and a stretcher that seemed too small to hold the greatness of you. They were careful and solemn as they wheeled you through the hallway of the orthopedic wing. Holly and I walked on either side of you, peering into the rooms of patients with new knees and hips...patients with new life.

There was a brief rush of cool, fresh air and a single ray of sunshine that fell across my face as I was lifted into the ambulance.

Holly and I drove behind you. There were no lights on the ambulance. No urgency for life. No rush to meet death.

I could sense my arrival at home. I looked out the window and said my last words.

The ambulance driver passed them on to us.

"My Oakley."

The sight of my tree brought me peace, like a balm for my weary eyes.

Dad had the hospital bed set up in the living room. Holly and I were upset that it wasn't faced toward the window, so that you could see Oakley. This seemed so important at the time...

...but it wasn't. There was nothing else for me to see in this lifetime, honey. Hospice had increased my morphine, and all I sensed through my physical form was the vibration of your familiar voices.

Hospice workers are angels on Earth. The nurses shared their knowledge and wisdom with firm authority and relentless compassion. Their directions were clear and their kindness was visceral. The aides cared for your body with swift, sure, and tender hands. You were their canvas as they washed and changed you and brushed your hair. One sang to you and another whispered sweet nothings (which were really *everythings*) in your ear. I have never witnessed more holy work.

I remember the singing. Was it "Amazing Grace?" No matter. It gave me a preview of Heaven.

•••

Mike and the kids came the next day, and Holly's Dave too. It was pouring down rain. An apt setting for this part of your movie.

I could feel everyone in the room. I tried to open my eyes and speak to the children, but I'm afraid what they saw and heard frightened them.

It wasn't fear they felt, Mom. It was dismay...mixed with the deepest sorrow they'd ever known. While your physical transformation was jarring for their young eyes, they were able to see you with their hearts. Because you taught them how to do that.

Yes, I guess I did.

We had quite a day all together.

It was as if I was in and out of my body at the same time. My senses were triggered intermittently. I smelled the hot dogs frying in butter on the stovetop... I never could pass up a hot dog! And I caught the pungent aroma of my favorite pasta from the local Italian restaurant.

The best pasta ever, right, Mom? We had all your favorites, including lots of potato chips, of course. It was a party for you, at least that's how we wanted the kids to experience it, a celebration of this journey you were completing.

I could feel the celebration...and the sadness underneath it.

Mike and I were working on a puzzle, a photograph of our whole happy family at a brewery in the mountains. This task was a perfect distraction from the harsh reality of the afternoon. We were looking for your smile...it was the missing piece. How could we have lost your dazzling smile? When Mike finally found it, his eyes welled with tears as he gently laid it in its place.

I could hear Grace and Holly in the kitchen talking about a concert. The effervescent intensity of their banter, like a crackling fire, made me feel warm. Rhode and Viv were in the basement watching TV, snuggled up with your dad on the sofa. Somehow I could see them...without seeing them.

I sat beside you and read aloud the last chapter of the last book we would share together...*The Tao of Pooh.*

You said I was your Pooh. True to you and to myself, unconcerned by that which I was not.

And I was your Piglet, always making sure of you, needing your validation at every turn.

These characters are both universal and familiar...

Holly is our Tigger, bouncing about with contagious enthusiasm. Sometimes I think she has a spring in her tail!

And your Dad, bless his heart, is our Rabbit, always seeking to solve the problem, to break the code...but cancer was a code he couldn't break, a code that, instead, broke part of him.

In your Pooh-like way, Mom, you showed all of us that there was nothing to solve, nothing to fix, nothing to do...but be.

The effort of seeking is futile, honey. Life unfolds through us, as us, regardless.

The image of you sleeping with the stuffed Pooh Bear tucked under your arm will stay with me forever. In your final days, you had fully returned to your innocence. You were in absolute harmony with Life.

At once, I was a little girl and an ancient woman. Pure and naked, yet layered with the wisdom of ages.

You had fulfilled your mission statement of this lifetime, Mom. You were a teacher of Truth simply by the way you showed up in the world.

Cancer allowed this fulfillment. It ripped through my outer layer to reveal my Light, my wholeness.

Thank you for showing us all of you, Pooh.

Thank you for seeing all of me, Piglet.

•••

As the sun went down, everyone gathered to hear the childhood stories you had dictated to me over the last months. What a privilege it was to be your voice, to read your words out loud.

Laughter conquered the sadness that had permeated the room. Even the kids were enthralled by my stories. The sentiment of the scene stirred me and made me want to stay, even though I knew it was time to go.

The best stuff of Life... against a backdrop of death.

The dogs were curled up in the middle of the circle you'd made around me. They were unusually calm, especially Happy. He knew. Dogs accept transition better than humans.

They were our greatest strength through those last days. They knew just when to offer us their comfort and when to distract us with their misbehavior.

There was plenty of misbehavior with those two. But it never really mattered to me.

For you, Mom, all that mattered was Love. And your relationship with your dogs was Love's most genuine reflection.

After the stories, I could feel the party coming to a close. I always lamented the end of a party. This one was no different. I sensed the weight of sadness returning to the room. I made a funny noise…and Vivi laughed.

I'm sorry you were aware of that, Mom.

What do you mean? I did it intentionally.

You did?

Yes! You adults were entirely too serious. You needed a child's laughter to release the tension!

I suppose we did.

Vivi's giggle provided the levity necessary for you and your sister and your dad to care for my failing body. It was all so unpleasant, so grave…

It was a comedy of errors, Mom. We tried to be tender and efficient like the hospice workers. Instead, we were like the three stooges.

It was an impossible situation, honey. You did the best you could. We all did.

•••

The next day, your breathing was slower, more labored. From what we could tell, the morphine was keeping your pain at bay.

There was no pain, just a longing to let go, an aching readiness. But my body was still so anchored to the Earth, to my family.

The Earth did love your dancing feet, Mom. Like us, it wasn't quite ready to release you.

I liked being in form, having a body to nurture and beautify. I'm not sure I would have been a content elderly person. For me, seventy-two years was a generous amount of time to be in a body. I danced a lot in seventy-two years.

Sitting beside you that day, I felt strangely serene. The body I was caring for was not you. Yet it was a gift to care for it, to discover the depth of my human compassion.

You and your sister and your dad were loving me into my transition, honey. Your resolve was the final permission I needed to fully relinquish my body to Spirit.

That night, Dad and Holly and I lit a candle and had dinner at the table not ten feet from your bed. Our dinnertime conversations that had been laced with the possibility of your recovery were replaced with talk of awful things. Obituaries, funerals, and gravestones. The words tasted like metal on our tongues. Dad mentioned putting your ashes in the graveyard on the hill. Knowing that this was not your wish, Holly and I exchanged defeated glances. I started to speak up…

…and I made the lights flicker.

We knew it was you, Mom. Speaking to us without words, through Light. A sacred sign of your formless brilliance...

…a rehearsal for my grand finale...

•••

I slept on the couch beside your bed that night. Your breathing was gurgling and grating, heavy and harsh. The alarm sounded every two hours, waking me from disturbed sleep to administer your morphine. At one o'clock in the morning, I remembered the date, December 19th. As I released the syringe of morphine into the side of your mouth, I told you it was Mike's birthday. That you could go. That he would hold us all up and together, as you had.

Dying on his birthday felt right in some odd way. An affirmation of our connection as mother and son, beyond blood. And an assurance that this day would hold more than sadness. With Mike, there is always joy.

I crawled back under my blanket, and through the window, I saw a shooting star. And then I heard the wild wind. The Christmas tree set up on the front porch was nearly carried away by the gusts, the angel ornaments flying from the evergreen branches.

Spirit finally came for me.

I looked over at you…and realized your silence. With weighted feet, I walked the three steps to your bedside. I put my hand on your cheek and you gasped. I ran upstairs to wake Holly, but she was already up. Awakened by the wind, by the knowing, by Spirit. We came down together to sit beside you. And then I can't remember. Holly says I left the room. And that you didn't breathe again. I thought we were both there to witness your final breath. I wish I could remember.

Grief distorts the mind, confirmation that thoughts don't really matter. Grasping for a memory, a perfect recollection of the past, is a hollow pursuit. All that matters, honey, is the Love present in each moment. And we've shared lifetimes of moments, lifetimes of Love.

Holly and I sat on either side of you, holding your hands. The wind, having come only to gather you, had ceased. The silence was paralyzing. Time had stopped.

From above my body, I watched you. And I stroked your hair. I whispered to your hearts that I was with you. That my Life continued…and our Love continued.

We woke Dad. While he made the necessary phone calls, Holly and I stepped outside. Winter had come. The wind that carried you away left a chill in its wake, so cold and raw that it hurt to breathe. The night sparkled with stars. Were they always this vivid? Their glare against the black sky made us squint. It was like being born. Born without a mother, unto ourselves, a noiseless wailing hanging in the stillness.

I heard your primal cry. And I cradled you as I had when you were born.

Back inside, I curled up beside you. But only for a moment. You were so cold. This body was not you. It felt wrong to lay beside this form that no longer contained you.

We were holding each other, Nicki Beans. There is no right or wrong in Love.

The funeral home workers arrived like characters out of a movie. So formal in their suits and ties, their top hats tipped toward us in sympathy. Did they really wear top hats? Moments later, the hospice nurse swooped in like an owl, wise and comforting. She removed your jewelry with sure and compassionate hands, and then signaled for the men to take you away. I don't remember you leaving, just that you were gone, in one horrific instant.

Not gone. I still am.

At Dad's request and with Holly's approval, I put on your wedding ring. It felt natural, yet heavy on my finger. I lay down on your bed and stared at my hand. Was it really my hand? Or was it still yours?

Your sister reached out to touch the ring on your finger, bringing you back to yourself. In my absence, she will always bring you back to yourself.

I roamed the house before finding myself curled up beside Holly in the upstairs bedroom, snuggled underneath the cream quilt, illuminated by the amber-tinted night light. In the wee hours of the morning, Holly got up to make juice. Because that's what you do when you lose your mother, she would say later, you remember the vitality of nature, of Life. You pull out all the vegetables from the refrigerator and you put them into the juicer that makes a horrible noise. A noise that drowns out your tears. You watch the orange and red and green liquid drip into the pitcher. And you marvel at the boldness of Life's color. When your mother dies, you make and drink juice.

Or you sleep, like I did, and dream dreams of shooting stars and wild wind and flying angels. And you awake to a tear-soaked pillow, a blindingly sunlit morning, and your sister's fresh juice.

If I did nothing else right as a mother, I raised you and your sister to love one another. Of this I am sure.

As I drank my juice, feeling the Life of it penetrate my tired cells, I opened my computer to type a note to all of your beloveds:

Nancy…is at Peace. Exquisite peace.
Peace be with you.
Love Always and Beyond…

After hitting the send button, I felt an urgent need to be home. I hugged Dad and Holly with all the strength I had left and then walked into a day that vibrated with mystery. The brightness of the sun made no sense. Didn't it know that it was shining on an empty world? On my way to the car, I think I saw a bluebird. I can't be sure. Regardless, in my head, I heard you singing…

"Mr. Bluebird's on my shoulder, it's the truth, it's actual, everything is satisfactual…"

I knew it was you.

•••

Mike and I planned to meet in the parking lot of a country church, just off the main road. A holy place that seemed fitting for this meeting. Here he would grab the metaphorical torch you had left for him. He would be with Dad on this most awful of days. He would help make the necessary arrangements. He would hold us all up and together…for you.

His promise.

He pulled up beside me as I stared blankly at the little white church, the words to the fingerplay I'd learned as a child looping through my mind… "This is the church, this is the steeple, open the doors…" I collapsed into my husband, pushing my head into his chest, willing his heart to open and enclose around me. On a day so cold, he was strangely warm. With eyes like crystal blue lakes, he spoke no words, allowing me to rest in the sanctuary of his arms for a moment of welcome fugue. Until I was ready to part from him. The drive home was a blur, like a tunnel through which only I was moving.

The angels were your guides.

When I arrived at home, I exhaled. Had I been holding my breath for sixty-six miles? I walked through the door to find my children sitting beside a roaring fire in the living room. Their faces were expectant and worried, their hands finding comfort in the thick coat of our chocolate lab. I told them about the star and the wind and the angels…and they hung onto my every word. Then they hung onto me.

Their first realization of impermanence and the inevitability of losing their mother.

I retreated to the shower, consoled by the spray of scalding hot water on dry winter skin. George, our lab, lay beside the shower stall, his nose making circles on the steamy glass. I could see the winter trees through the window, naked and cold. Were they sad too, I wondered?

I needed to be among the trees. At the river. With my dog and my children.

I dressed quickly, catching a glimpse of you in the mirror. Had I always looked this much like you? Our noses differ, mine bulbous and crooked, yours pointed and straight. But there you were in my reflection.

I've always been in your reflection…and you in mine.

Downstairs, I found the girls still by the fire. Rhode was gone, off playing with friends, the intensity of the day too much for an eleven-year-old boy to bear.

Your pain was too much for him to bear.

My daughters were eager to please. And eager to be with me. We loaded George in the back of the minivan and headed out, waving with detached hands at happy neighbors putting up Christmas lights.

Life on Earth goes on…

Through the woods, over the bridge, down the steps, we made our way to the river. A few leaves fell from the almost barren trees, an offering of sweet sympathy and a reminder that all things will eventually die.

All things transform, honey. Death is an illusion.

George was in his own Heaven—the freedom to run and explore, to smell peculiar scents and swim in frigid water. I wondered if you were experiencing this kind of joy in your Heaven.

Oh, yes. I had fallen into the arms of my mom and dad and so many other souls who had loved and been loved by me. There was overwhelming relief...and yes, absolute joy.

I'm so glad, Mom. As I walked behind my precious girls, I thought of the powerful trine that you and Holly and I formed. The three of us were such a force together, everyone said so.

And now, you are creating the foundation for another trine— transitioning from daughter and baby sister...to mother and matriarch.

I wondered if I had the maternal maturity and vision to make this trine as beautifully united as the first. Could I ever be the kind of mother that you were to Holly and me?

At once, in my mind's eye, I saw my daughters' and my first initials—G V N. And I heard the answer to my question in your voice…

It's a GiVeN.

I built two cairns, side by side. Both with three stones.

A shrine of two trines...

Sitting on a rock, I watched Grace and Viv throw sticks across the water for George to fetch. The sunlight bounced off the rolling river to create a celestial setting. My girls glanced over at me every few moments, smiling their radiant smiles, assuring me of their presence, their love.

Your trine.

On our way out, we met a family—grandparents, parents, and two boys. The youngest was celebrating his first birthday. His name was Nathaniel.

An "N" name. Of course.

Nathaniel means, "gift from God."

A gift for you. A death day. A birthday. Both a testament to everlasting Life.

•••

I asked Dad and Holly if I could write your obituary. I knew it would be both a challenge and an honor to capture your genius on paper. You were anything but customary and it was important that your obituary mirrored your unique essence. This was about you—not the people you left behind.

Here it is. My colorful life...in black and white.

> Nancy Ruth Schellinger Rhode crossed over into the Light on Saturday, December 19, 2015 at her home in Scottsville, Virginia.
>
> Her legacy of unyielding love lives on in her husband of fifty years, her children, grandchildren, sister, niece, nephew, animals, and friends. While her life's work would reflect an array of achievements in the areas of retail, interior design, geriatric care, volunteerism, and the arts, what defined and drove Nancy could not easily be put on paper.
>
> Nancy was her relationships. Connecting with others and uniting the mind and heart were her passions and her gifts. Nancy was altruism; bestowing unseen kindnesses upon strangers was her routine. Nancy was wisdom, seeking deeper spiritual understanding in her quest to teach and inspire others was her basic instinct. Nancy was beauty. And she brought it to Light in every room she decorated, in every ensemble she orchestrated, in every animal she nurtured, and in every human being she loved. The harmony and unity she manifested on Earth will live on in everything and everyone she touched.

Yes. This. Thank you, honey.

On the morning it was printed, I opened the paper with trembling hands. Seeing your name and picture was incomprehensible—what were you doing on this page, among all these sad stories? Nancy, with the laughing face, you should be in the Lifestyles section modeling the latest fashions. Not here in section B, on page 4.

I wasn't there. A reflection of my life was there. I was perched on your shoulder, reading your lovely words along with you.

So many reached out with condolences, Mom. Friends I haven't seen since childhood wrote to share their memories of you. Remember Susan Wilson?

Of course I remember Susan.

She recalled a tender moment when you scooped her up after a fall. She had ripped the orange sweatpants we'd let her borrow. She was worried you'd be upset, yet all you revealed was genuine concern for her well-being.

That little Susan was always falling down, bless her heart. I loved being a mother to you and Holly, and also to your friends. Offering a smile, a hug, a kind word, comfort after a fall. The most trivial gestures foster the deepest impressions.

In the weeks following your passing, it seemed every person I encountered took the time to really see and love me, if only for a moment. An acquaintance from high school stopped me in a crowded restroom at the movie theater. She placed her hand on my arm and looked into my eyes, the sound of running water and hand driers drowning out any words she may have said. All I could sense was her compassion, her willingness to pause from the business of life to rest with me in my sadness.

A moment of Love. Simple and profound.

One day I came home to find a basket of fairy house offerings on my doorstep—a gift of whimsy assembled by friends who knew that building a fairy house is what you do when your mother dies.

Affirmation that your friends do indeed see and love you, honey.

A poem by Naomi Shihab Nye helped me understand the sisterhood of sorrow and kindness...

> "Before you know kindness as the deepest thing inside,
> you must know sorrow as the other deepest thing."

Yes, the deepest of human things—sorrow and kindness.

•••

Mike couldn't endure our sorrow, and the greatest kindness he could extend was an all-inclusive vacation to the Caribbean. He surprised us on Christmas Eve. He said he got a deal. He didn't. Who gets a deal on a last minute trip to paradise the day after Christmas? For him, regardless of our finances, this kindness—for all of us to be away together—was the only thing that made sense.

I'm glad you didn't argue with him.

I didn't have the energy to argue.

Sometimes you have to let go…and let Mike.

On the flight to St. Lucia, stuck on the runway for an hour, Holly made friends with the pilot and hung out in the galley with the crew.

Our Tigger!

The kids were plugged into their various devices and Mike was reading behind his sunglasses. I was writing, the words I would share at your service the following month.

You are always so busy, so focused. You've got some Rabbit in you, Nicki Beans.

Sometimes I don't know what I think before I write it. And like Rabbit, I'm uncomfortable with the unknown.

In your effort to figure it all out, honey, you not only exhaust yourself, but you miss out on the beauty of just being in the moment, in the mystery.

Accepting the mystery is a tall order for Rabbit, Mom. As I watched our Tigger flirting with the pilot, I wished for more levity in my life. But in reality, we were all just seeking refuge from our pain. Mike in his shot of bourbon and a mystery novel, Holly in her connection with strangers, the kids with their social media, me with my words.

Avoiding pain is what humans do. The heart can only hold so much. But pain is demanding. And sitting intimately with it is the only way it will release its grip on you. Grief calls for a balance of distraction and surrender.

Just before takeoff, I dug through my purse to find the ultimate distraction, in the form of a little blue pill. Valium allowed me the escape

I desperately needed from my grief. As I slid into sedation, I stared out the window, sure I was very close to Heaven up here at forty thousand feet. Certainly, if I looked hard enough or allowed my gaze to blur, I would see you.

I was right beside you.

But I couldn't see you! And I feared I would never see or hear you again. Who was Piglet without his Pooh? It was lonely in the clouds, Mom.

And so you slept...and found me in your dreams.

Yes.

Until the wheels came down in paradise.

Well, not quite. The guests who had been at our resort for a while called it a five-star dump...but it was our dump for four days, and we mightily embraced the Life of it, the Life of us.

Through the sunshine, I smiled on you.

We felt you, Mom....as the kids and I ate our weight in french fries, and Holly and Mike drank their weight in margaritas. The all-inclusive experience offered us unlimited distractions from our grief, but our sadness was ever-present. Tears spilled on every shiny, happy scene of the trip.

I danced with you and Holly in the lobby of the hotel. A reggae band was playing and you girls were in your joy, even with tears rolling down your sunburned cheeks. You were holding it all.

Because you were holding us, Mom. "Looking in your Big Brown Eyes" was the song, and we were all doing just that. Your brown eyes were glistening with ours. Your lips were pursed and you were shaking that cute bottom of yours...

I am a good dancer. Always have been. When I was in high school, all the boys wanted to be my partner.

I bet they did!

You got some of my moves, honey...but not all of them.

•••

Back home, we re-entered reality as best we could. Holly and I made the trek to Idylwood to help Dad sort through your things. My goodness, Mom, you had a lot of clothes!

Oh boy, here we go. I know I had a lot of clothes. And perhaps my spending habits were a bit excessive.

A bit.

Well, you and many others certainly benefited from my hand-me-downs.

It gave you such pleasure to make other people beautiful too.

Yes, it did. And this day was no different. What a fashion show you and your sister put on for me! I taught you well.

We were searching for church clothes, funeral clothes. Which was a challenge in your closet. Your style could be best described as shabby chic meets sexy classic… and only you could pull off your look for church.

I loved marching to my own beat down the aisle of the sanctuary. God loved it too, I think.

We channeled you the next day, Mom. We marched into the church, decked out in *Nancy*, to talk to Randy about the upcoming service, your celebration of Life.

Your dad was kind, deferring to you and your sister to make most of the decisions. His eyes looked tired and gray. I could feel his heartache under his cloak of composure.

I was too overwhelmed by my own feelings to consider his too, Mom. I'm sorry. My inner child emerged with petulant force. In response to one innocent mention of Jesus, I said, "This isn't about Jesus, this is about my mom."

You and your sister knew my buttons around religious doctrine. Dad and Randy heard you and respected your thoughts about the different components of the service.

And it was a beautiful service, Mom.

Let me tell it.

Your celebration. Your story.

The date was set for Saturday, January 23rd. A few days prior, the weather forecast for the weekend made headline news… "possibly the biggest blizzard to hit Virginia since 1996!"

Since my wedding day. January 6, 1996.

The most sacred things happen in the snow, honey. You sent out a note to my friends.

> Dear Friends,
>
> We want to let everyone know that Saturday's service will go on—snow or shine. This feels very resonant of our blizzard wedding twenty years ago. Mom is smiling for sure. That said, we know it could be difficult, maybe even impossible, to get here. And the last thing Mom would want is for anyone to be unsafe.
>
> So, I woke up this morning with a vision of circles—maybe sixty-six of them—intimate groups gathering through the winter to honor Mom and to allow the seeds of wisdom she planted in so many—to grow.
>
> We see Circles everywhere—my house, Holly's house, Idylwood, maybe your house? Mom wouldn't want just one service…she would want a whole series! Holly is calling it the "Mama Movement!"
>
> AND THEN…we will have a brilliant party in the spring—Nancy style—dancing around her Gratitude Garden and loving each other up! Stay tuned for those details.
>
> On Saturday morning, please light a candle at eleven o'clock, and hold our mom in your heart. We will feel you in ours.

The snow began falling on Friday afternoon. Vivi was dancing out on the sidewalk when Holly and Dave pulled up to your house. Holly looked just like me and Vivi told her so. Holly beamed. Mike took Dave and Rhode in the Jeep, and you and Holly and the girls followed in the SUV. A caravan of Love through the falling snow. The roads were getting slick so the angels traveled with you.

I could feel their wings, Mom. We arrived at Idylwood and gathered what we needed to set up for the service—mementos, candles, flowers...and a case of Budweiser in case we got thirsty.

In case Mike got thirsty. My boy loves his Bud.

Right.

The four of you drove down the winding lane to the church. This was no place to be during a blizzard, but the show had to go on!

And what a show it would be!

I watched you all trudge through the snow with boxes of my treasures and bushels of ice-kissed daisies. Inside, you turned on my soundtrack, my favorite songs of all time. You transformed the parish hall into a little slice of Heaven! My pictures, my books, my stones, my love letters...and "Nancy's Playground," where my divination cards and runes were laid out to be explored. Holly lit dozens of candles and the place was illuminated...with me.

We put your face up on the big screen! We all got lost in the slideshow and the music. "Brown Eyed Girl" was playing when Dave wondered aloud, "What if she walked in now and started advising us on the placement and flow of the room...what if she walked in right now?" We laughed and cried and ate the butter cookies that were meant for the next day.

When your mother dies, you laugh and cry and eat butter cookies.

It was dusk when we left the church, and the snow was coming down hard. Mike drove us slowly through the dancing flakes. Mesmerized by the mystery, he came to a stop in the middle of the lane. "How did we get here?" he asked of no one and everyone.

You were parked in front of a farm named "Mount Gallant." Holly said this was an appropriate place to pause...because I was gallant—brave and bold and heroic. I liked that.

We all piled out of the truck and looked up into the magic of the falling sky. Holly and I plopped down on the ground to make snow angels, Mom angels. Our fingers touched as we flapped our wings, your wings. The cold was comforting—like a wake-up call to your voice,

I still am... Feel me.

We felt you, Mom, in the snow...and in the passion of Mike's rant.

My Michael. With his anger rising and the vein at his temple pulsing, he reported on the texts coming in from friends, all the regrets from people unable to attend my service.

"This is no time to be reasonable," he screamed at the sky. "This is the stuff for which we risk it all. These are the experiences that define us!"

He is such a loyal protector of this family.

Just like you, Mom.

Just like me. You took a group selfie in the snow—each of you so brilliantly yourselves and so connected to each other. You couldn't get close enough. "Squeeze in," Mike said, less for the picture than for the sensation of touch, the reminder of Love.

We made it home for a happy hour by the fire. It didn't feel happy. The bourbon bestowed a blissful burn, masking the ache in my chest. I had to escape the warmth of the house. It was suffocating. I retreated to the darkness of the woods, the full moon's reflection on the snow showed me the way. There was no visible life, the animals all hiding in their nests and burrows. It was piercingly still.

I was there.

I felt you, Mom. Back inside, we watched a home video of a family vacation in the mountains. "Hiiiiiii..." you sang, waving to the camera, a forest of trees behind you. You were so alive. None of this made sense.

You spent the night in my office, my sanctuary for meditation, yoga, list-making.

I stared out the window and watched the moonbeams dance their way through the naked trees and onto the altar of your ashes and the paintings of your parents. My grandparents.

You were held in the legacy of your ancestors' Light, your birthright.

And surrounded by your books, your notes…and ladybugs, crawling all over the window sills and baseboards. Symbols of joy…and Truth.

What better message for this new landscape of your life and our Love. Thank you, ladybugs.

•••

I slept in your robe, your embrace. And woke to a world covered in white, your favorite color. I went outside and said, with absurdity, "Show me a sign, Mom."

"What more do you want"? I quipped.

I heard you. I looked up into the sky and laughed, catching the snow on my tongue and a poem on my heart.

Snow,
Falling from Heaven,
A mere moment of grace
And purity.
Only to blend,
Then melt
Into exquisite emptiness
And everythingness…

I dressed in your clothes. And used your makeup brush to caress my face.

Like I would have with the back of my hand. You looked beautiful. You looked like me.

I walked through the house chanting, "Okay, okay, okay…" I began to worry, what if nobody comes?

I inspired you with a vision.

A vision of Happy, your beloved dog, walking down the aisle of the sanctuary. It wouldn't matter if no one else came as long as the whole family, including the crazy golden retriever, was there to celebrate you.

Nothing matters but Love, honey, and Happy is Love. Golden Love.

I knew this was your idea, Mom. While I love Happy, his neurotic behavior leaves a lot to be desired. But planning for his presence at your service was the only thing that made sense on this snowy morning.

You shared this revelation with your dad, who sighed at first...

We all know that signature sigh!

...but then conceded upon receiving Randy's gracious response to the request, "Of course Happy should come. He's on the program."

What a perfect picture for the program, Mom...you and your cherished animal!

On the way to the church, the car was quiet. Suddenly, Rhode exclaimed, "Look!"

A deer. That was me. Gentle, innocent, the embodiment of Life's mysteries.

Fitting that Rhode saw you first.

There are no coincidences.

At the church, neighbors and parishioners were shoveling walkways and preparing food in the parish hall. Your friends Chris and Denise walked a mile through the snow to celebrate you, to comfort us. "This is where we want to be," they said.

The quaint sanctuary was like a scene out of Little House on the Prairie. The big windows, the old pews, the tiny balcony where Dave sat strumming his guitar. My baby picture and my daisies bathed in the Light of the three candles on the altar. Such elegant beauty.

62

Such a reflection of you.

The Breens pulled up, all the way from the beach. "Wouldn't miss this," they said. Then the Cushnies came—George was on crutches after foot surgery!

A few others trickled in to fill the space. But still the sanctuary felt so empty. I stood by the window, fogging up the glass with my sorrow.

And just in time, down the snow-covered lane rolled the people for whom I knew your heart was waiting. Your best friends.

Kristen came in first... I fell into her Virgo arms and then kissed the cheeks of her sweet little girls. A moment later, the wind carried Patrick through the doors, followed by Jerry in his three-piece suit, covered in snow, "Wild horses couldn't keep us away, Nic."

And Mike echoed, "No time to be reasonable."

We took our places in the first pew. Happy meandered down the aisle, stopping to be stroked by kind hands before finding his resting place at Dad's feet. We listened to Randy's words of welcome. Then we stood, Holly and Grace and I, in front of the small yet mighty congregation. You were with us, Mom.

I was with and in all of you, including my Happy. You painted such poignant pictures of my life and told stories in my voice, allowing my resonance to enter the infinite heart space of those gathered. You honored me more deeply than I could have dreamed.

In the exhale of our remembrances we sang "Amazing Grace." My Grace, not one for physical affection, slid close to Dad and leaned into him, filling the void of your absence as best she could.

"How precious did that Grace appear the hour I first believed..."

Randy's words were precious too—a message from Jesus, a message from you...

"Love one another, as I have loved you."

And then we walked as One from the sanctuary, through the winter wonderland, to the parish hall.

Rhode and Viv led the way, carrying my picture and my daisies. Happy followed, pausing to add some color to the snow.

He made us laugh, as if it was his job. Inside, we gathered in a circle.

I love a circle.

Happy took the napkins from the table and offered them to our friends, as though he knew tears would be falling.

That's my Happy.

We passed the flame, candle to candle to candle...and Randy invited each of us to share a word that reflected your essence, your imprint on us.

I love this game!

Mike started with a story.

I love Mike's stories!

He told about one of our many family trips, this one to Cabo San Lucas.

Oh dear.

The time you had too many margaritas…

It was the ice, honey!

...and Mike had to carry you home.

Never drink the water in Mexico. It was the ice, I tell you.

His word was *TOGETHER*. And through tears, he said,

"I'm going to miss traveling with you."

The other words shared were profound. I wish I could remember them all. I did tuck my children's words into my heart, so that I might retrieve them should they ever forget…

Viv said,

"JOYFUL."

Grace offered,

"BIG."

And Rhode whispered,

"COLORFUL."

I'll never forget.

Somehow, I got the honor of closing the circle. I didn't know what I was going to say until the moment the word found itself on my lips.

"PROMISE."

It was your "word of the year," your intention for 2012, and I'd had it engraved on a key for you, a key I happened to be wearing around my neck on this snowy day. A remembrance of every promise we've made to each other across lifetimes... and a prophecy of the promise we'd yet to make, the promise of this book.

Yes. This book. Our promise.

•••

After the circle, it was time to celebrate!

My movie! My music! My playground!

There was Brunswick stew and ham biscuits and salmon. Jerry brought a cooler of beer.

Jerry is a traveling party.

And there was lots of red wine. Some splattered on the walls.

The sign of a good time... I made my mark in the parish hall!

It was an intimate affair. Everyone drew one of your divination cards, a message that seemed to come from you, from beyond.

I made sure everyone got the reminder of Love that they needed.

There were so many stories, so much appreciation for your life, Mom. And there were questions...

I love questions!

People wanted more of you, as if you were a story that had ended too soon.

That's what we're doing now, honey. We're continuing the story... together.

Just like Mike said. Together...

•••

While most of our friends couldn't be with us, we certainly felt their devotion, their candescence. Absently checking my phone, I found two videos in my inbox. One featured all the candles lit across my neighborhood during your service. And one held my precious friends, illuminated by Love and singing my favorite song, "This Little Light of Mine."

"Let it shine, let it shine, let it shine..."

Later we received a book put together by our dearest ones, commemorating all the Light summoned that day—in memory of you.

The sisterhood of kindness and sorrow.

Mike finally gave up his grudge. "More than reasonable," he conceded.

Ah, the transformative power of Light. I may not be shining in the world now, but I am shining on it.

Throughout the winter, even on the coldest days, Holly and I felt your warmth, your ever-presence. And we got busy with "The Mama Movement."

A vision of circles...

Something magical happens when people come together in a circle. They connect more deeply with themselves, with each other...and over time, this translates to their connection with the world.

Everything natural and beautiful is a circle—the sun, the moon, the earth, the seasons, the cycle of life. All turning round and round...

People thought Holly and I were doing too much, that we needed to rest. But gathering people together, in your honor, was part of our grieving process. We needed the movement of the circle to move us through our grief.

You brought me back to my friends, illuminating the potential for relationship beyond death... and the Truth of eternal Love.

•••

We decided to take the Mama Movement on the road, or rather, through the air!

This is a great story. You tell it.

Nearly three months after you passed, Holly and I planned a trip back to our roots, back to Cincinnati. We wanted to return you to the city that raised you by spreading your ashes around the tree that shaded your parents' graves. Since it's illegal to bring ashes on an airplane, Holly put you in a vitamin and mineral powder bag. She thought she could pass you off as a health supplement. Metaphorically, you were the embodiment of the Genesis Complex, a product that touts, "...love is the primordial energy of existence."

How wonderful!

Of course, the bag of this white powdery substance caused alarm in the security line at the airport, and Holly was pulled for questioning.

You girls! You know, when I traveled, they always pulled me from the security line at the airport too. I must have looked sneaky.

No, Mom, you looked like a movie star. They just wanted a closer look at you. But on this day, you looked like a big bag of cocaine.

Oh, your sister was loving the adventure of this.

She was, while I sat on the bench behind her chanting, "Help, Mom," under my breath for the five-minute eternity in the purgatory of the airport. As the the security guard prepared the test that is performed on questionable substances, Holly answered his inquiries with her signature breezy grace. "Yes, this powder is more granular than most, but it dissolves easily in water… No, it's not outrageously expensive, it's comparable in price to other powders on the market… Yes, it does give me more energy and mental clarity." Throughout the investigation, Holly kept looking over her shoulder at me for confirmation, "It's the best stuff ever, right, Nic?"

The best stuff ever…the best stuff of Life.

You girls!

In the end, the security guard wrote down the name of the product. He planned to buy some for his wife.

Oh dear.

You see, Mom, you continue to teach and inspire wherever you go.

I certainly do.

Cincinnati greeted us with a morning that was moist and cool. It was still winter, heavy and penetrating, but there was a faint scent of spring in the air, a scent of hope and new beginnings. We drove to the cemetery, a vast landscape of green hills and resting places. We must have walked a million steps looking for Grandma and Grandpa…traversing countless gravestones, pausing intermittently and respectfully to ponder a life lived, a death grieved.

Finally, Holly found them...Alma Louisa Carolina Schellinger and
Richard Paul Schellinger. Their names, set in stone, under a small but
sturdy tree.

I knelt down, my knees immediately soaked by the wet grass, and kissed
their stones. I breathed you into the scene.

I was already there. We all were...the five of us, our star of 66.

Yes. Our star of 66.

Tell that story, honey. The undeniable affirmation of our soul connection.

•••

About fifteen years ago, I stood on the beach gazing out upon the winter
ocean. The violent wind unsettled me, unleashing big questions around
the randomness of Life. In the face of fear, I summoned my inner Rabbit
to find some order, some control over the uncontrollable. My busy brain
did not disappoint, offering me comfort in the form of a number.

66.

It occurred to me that my birthday and your birthday were 66 days apart,
and your birthday and Holly's birthday were also 66 days apart.
Incidentally, Holly was born in 1966. This not only confirmed our
connection as a trine, but also the existence of sweet order in the
Universe. I was elated with this new knowing...but, as usual, only
temporarily satisfied.

Your brain is never satisfied, Nicki Beans.

True, but in this case, I felt less neurotic and more curious, as though
Spirit was transmitting critical information and I best pay attention. With
little effort, my calculations revealed that my sister's and my grandma's
birthdays were also 66 days apart, as were my grandma's and grandpa's
birthdays.

Wickedly cool discovery, huh, Mom?

Wickedly cool, honey.

Here are the dates, if you want to check my math:

July 14
September 18
November 23
January 28
April 4

Years later, I realized that my middle child missed the next "66" by one day. However, it should be noted that her name is Vivi. VI + VI= 66. There are no coincidences, right, Mom?

Right, honey. I'll never forget the day that little one was born. Even in menopause, I bled as I witnessed Vivi's birth. We were so linked—body, mind, and soul. We still are.

She has your big, beautiful head, Mom, and your adorable toes.

The pinky toe that curls under. She can't deny me.

When you got sick, another insight came to me in a dream. I awoke trembling, remembering the deaths of my beloved grandparents, two of the points on our star of 66. Grandma and Grandpa both died at age 72. Grandma died when I was 14 and she was born in 1914. Grandpa died when I was 15 and he was born in 1915.

At the time of this epiphany, you were two months shy of your 72nd birthday. And I was about to turn 43, the same age you were when your mom died.

I was born in 1943.

And I was born…in 1972.

I know that was hard to hold, honey.

While I initially received this dream as a nightmare, the more conscious part of me leaned into the gift and profound prophecy of it. How could I fear this message delivered with Love from beyond? How could I refuse this reminder of the sacred contract we made in no-time, before incarnating in our separate forms?

An agreement made in Spirit's gentle embrace.

Certainly, Holly and I did not let this revelation overshadow your will to live or our efforts to keep you with us. We hoped beyond measure that your body would heal and you would break the cycle your parents initiated.

It was too much work. I was tired and ready to go Home.

In the end, your destiny of seventy-two years as Nancy Schellinger Rhode was sealed.

It was a beautiful life. What more could I have possibly wanted?

66 and 72. Birth and death. The full circle of Life…and Love.

•••

At the cemetery, Holly and I dug our hands into the bag of your ashes, letting our fingers play with the earth of you. Like children in a sandbox, we delighted in this sensory experience. So tactile. So human.

Ashes to ashes, dust to dust…

We sprinkled you around the tree and the stones, filling the letters that formed your parents' names…with you. A whimsical expression of your return to them. Then we played, throwing the ashes in the air and allowing them to rain down on us. We were covered in you.

My children in my sandbox.

Holly went to find our great-grandparents' gravestones. To make an offering of your ashes to our ancestors.

My wise Holly.

An ache rose up in my head, heavy and gnawing. A reminder of my humanity. The burden of physical pain.

So you climbed the tree that shaded your grandparents' resting place. My little fairy in her tie-dyed pants.

I wanted to fly away, Mom. To leave my blood and bones behind. I wanted to be with you.

In time, you will be, Nicki Beans. Now is not that time.

Holly found me in the tree. Like always, she brought me back to myself and to this reality. We held hands on our way to the car and left our suffering in the cemetery. Then we drove...across the memories you made in Cincinnati.

•••

In the months that followed your death, I looked for you in everything. I walked your walk in your boots and danced your dance with your scarves. I spent hours playing with your beauty products and smelling your lotions, breathing you into me.

You stared into the mirror that you bordered with sticky note wisdom...

...hearing your voice in those words and searching for your face in mine. The mirror was a portal to you. Yet nowhere were you more present than in meditation.

You found mercy in meditation.

You were a tree growing inside of me, your roots embedded in the seat of my soul, your face a wooden mask over mine, uncarved. Your branches erupting from my crown into the Light.

Your feet firmly planted in the earth of me.

And my spirit with you in Heaven.

We walked like a prayer between worlds.

Together...

...for always...

•••

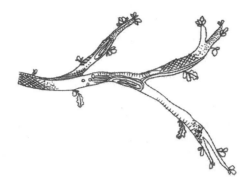

Spring

...

It's spring, Mom. The season of birth and rebirth. The seeds you planted in me are bursting with promise. Let's rise and howl with the joy of Life!

Let's go outside and play, Nicki Beans. Can you smell the honeysuckle on the breeze?

It smells like Heaven. It smells like you. Let's lounge in the soft grass and make flower crowns.

Don't forget the daisies, honey.

I could never forget the daisies, Mom.

Look at Oakley... He's waking up slowly from his long rest, his delicate buds emerging from his mighty branches. Good morning, Oakley! Good morning, beauty!

Your gratitude garden is awakening too...the tulips rising from the Earth, stretching toward Heaven, inviting us to celebrate Life. It's time for a party.

A party! I love a party.

Well, this is a big one. A couple hundred people are coming to honor you, Mom. We've got a band and food and party favors…a rainbow of daisies, a rainbow of you.

My goodness. What will you wear?

A very important question.

It is. We decorate the world with our clothes, honey. What we wear tells the story of our essence, our creative spirit.

Your granddaughters and I will be wearing white… Holly insisted on animal print.

My angels and my wolf. Your stories. You are animated art!

And we're all wearing the flower crowns we made together. We are One with spring, One with you. Here come your people, Mom…

Oakley is welcoming them. Idylwood is coming back to Life!

Holly is leading the crowd in a sing-along of our favorite Carpenters hit… "Top of the World."

> *"Not a cloud in the sky, got the sun in my eyes*
> *And I won't be surprised if it's a dream…"*

There are lots of tears in this dream, Mom, but lots of laughter too.

I'm in all of it.

Yes, you are. I don't want it to be over.

Nothing really ends, honey... It just transforms into something else. Life is but a series of moments that unfold one after another. You take the memories of the precious moments we've shared in this lifetime and you allow Spirit to fold them into this new thing…this book we're writing now.

It's never really over. I like that, Mom.

•••

Let's sit in the gratitude garden and tell each other our springtime stories.

We'll have to go back to Cincinnati, where it all began.

Our hearts will take us there...back to the day Nancy Schellinger came into this world.

My mom's contractions started in the afternoon. She was in the bathroom when her neighbor Elsie came over and said, "Alma, that baby's going to come out in the toilet." Mom called Daddy at work and he drove up Edgewood Avenue like a flash. When they got to the hospital, I was already crowning. I was quick my whole seventy-two years...until I had to slow down in those final days. But on that day, September 18, 1943—boom! There I was, all nine pounds and six ounces of me. I had a big head even then, but Mom had the hips to birth me...

You did *not* have the hips to birth me, Mom. I was a caesarean section baby, scheduled to enter the world a week before my due date. To this day, I love a schedule. Grandma and Grandpa stayed with Holly, who, after five and a half years of being an only child, was less than elated by the prospect of me. You and Dad went to Dairy Queen on your way to the big event. You got a cake cone with chocolate ice cream. Upon arriving at the hospital, you plopped down in a wheelchair and, with reckless abandon, Dad steered you through the hallways shouting, "This woman is having a baby!" Even though it was your childhood dream to have six boys, you were thrilled when the doctor said, "It's a girl!" You left the hospital with me next to your heart, my happiest place then...and now.

That's right, Nicki Beans. That was a happy, happy day...

•••

What was your first house like, Mom?

We lived on Edgewood Avenue in a yellow brick house with brown and cream awnings. The house sat on top of a hill in Winton Place—a small, German, blue-collar community where you didn't have to go far to find one of your relatives. There was a bus stop, a grocery store, three churches, and a beauty shop where Mom had her hair done once a week.

Because hair is power.

Yes, my mom taught me that. I loved our little neighborhood. We walked everywhere. There was never a shortage of kids who wanted to play, whether it was a kickball game in the street or a game of jacks on someone's front porch. We never locked our doors, although Daddy thought we should when he was gone. Mom liked the house wide open. She was proud of her house...proud of her decorating. The wall leading upstairs had black wallpaper with big pink flowers on it. That kind of sophistication was unique back then. Mom just smiled when anyone complimented her good taste. With open doors and open hearts, she and Daddy would say "Come on in..." to anyone passing by. Being at our house gave people a good feeling. My parents gave people a good feeling.

Holly and I visited Winton Place and your home on the hill after you passed. As we walked the streets of your old neighborhood, you were with us, showing us the magic of your childhood.

Back then, there was genuine appreciation for the little things. Saturday nights were big deals, just getting together with other families, taking turns at different houses. We had potato chips and soda pop while we listened to the radio. It was all so wonderful! Sometimes I fell asleep and had to be carried home. Usually we walked to these gatherings, but occasionally we had to drive. Daddy probably drank too much to have been behind the wheel. He had a lot of fire in him and often drove too fast. I liked when he called me Curly Top, when I could feel the softness of him, under his rough exterior.

I had a curly top too, Mom. My childhood memories began in Reynoldsburg, Ohio, on Twilight Drive, a flat block of middle America with sidewalks and starter homes and manicured front lawns. Like most women in the seventies, you stayed home with us. Our days were filled with Candy Land, coloring books, and *Captain Kangaroo.* The mothers would sit in a circle on the front lawn, chatting and smoking, while the children raced through their legs in endless games of hide and seek. Most every night was spent curled up on the brown and orange plaid couch watching *Happy Days* or singing along with Donny and Marie Osmond on the television. Like Grandma, you loved to decorate. You were delighted with the white sofa and blue velvet chairs you purchased for the living room. "For adults only," you warned. You did a lot of entertaining in that room. Did you know that Holly and I used to sit on the stairs and watch you, relaxing on the fancy couch with your martini, commanding the attention of your guests with your infectious smile? Even as little girls, we were mesmerized by your charm.

My beautiful little girls...

When I was six years old, you and Dad announced that we would be moving to Virginia. You said Dad was climbing the ladder at Xerox, which I took literally. He's climbing a ladder to Virginia? I remember thinking that was an odd name for a state. But I was excited about the idea of a new house...until I realized we would be leaving behind my best friend, Julie.

I can see us there in the twilight of the last day we spent on Twilight Drive. The moving van packed and the house locked, our sad neighbors surrounding the old, wood-paneled station wagon, wishing us safe travels and happy times in Virginia. You and Julie, each holding your treasured stuffed animals, shared a tearful embrace, then waved to each other as we pulled away.

That moment held my first taste of grief...but children are resilient. It didn't take long for me to dry my tears and begin my car acrobatics, flipping back and forth between the back seat and the way back seat until I fell asleep, much to the relief of my big sister.

Bless her twelve-year-old, broken heart. Leaving the familiarity of her middle school friends and her first boyfriend...

Italian Tony! She loved that boy. She loved Twilight Drive. She didn't want to leave.

Yet she hid her pain from us, as if there wasn't room for it in our family dynamic. Like your grandma and me, Holly always wore a smile for the greater good. In this case, for the peaceful transition to our new life in Virginia.

For me, the well-being of the collective was secondary to my own inner peace. Like tidal waves, my emotions were a force I couldn't contain. If I had a strong feeling, everyone around me was going to feel it too.

Your sister allowed the space for you to fully express yourself. She honored the changing tides of you, often at the expense of her own natural ebb and flow.

She loved me that much.

She continues to love you that much.

After our eight-hour journey, the station wagon finally made the turn onto Farnham Drive. With beaming pride, you pointed to our new home on the top of the hill, perhaps remembering your own childhood home on the top of the hill. Holly gushed at the beauty of it and, in true form, I shrieked, "It's yellow! Who lives in a yellow house?"

We always knew what was on your mind, Nicki Beans. I told you it was mustard, not yellow.

Which seemed even stranger. A mustard house? With red shutters?

They were burgundy shutters, honey.

"Weird," I whispered loudly to my stuffed dog Henry, making sure everyone in the car could hear. The mustard anomaly was huge in comparison to our home in Ohio. And the neighborhood, with its rolling hills and expansive yards, was the perfect setting for the fairytale of my sweet and sheltered childhood.

The summers were enchanted. Every day began the same... I jumped out of bed and into my swim team bathing suit, threw a towel around my neck, chugged a glass of juice, hopped on my star princess-themed bike with the indigo-blue banana seat, and glided down Farnham Hill— friends by my side, wind in my hair, and infinite possibilities for the day looping through my mind. The hours unfolded naturally after swim team practice... My pals and I sat on the diving board and sucked the sugar off Fun Dip sticks for energy we told ourselves we needed. Then we cruised by the tennis courts to get water from the big, orange cooler—the novelty of those paper cone cups never wore off. Sometimes I stopped by Kerry's house for an official meeting of the Hunga Bunga club (of which we were the only members), before returning home to play jungle queen on the rope swing in our backyard.

At noon, you called me in for lunch. We ate peanut butter on Wonder bread (mine with jelly, yours with mayonnaise), while watching *The Price is Right* streaming through the little black and white television on the kitchen counter. Then you went back to your chores and I went back to the pool. Sometimes you came with me and sat on the side, dangling your feet in the water so that I could play with your toes and do flips between your legs. You always left too soon, the responsibility of homemaking calling you back to Farnham Drive.

I enjoyed my chores, especially my time in the kitchen with my recipe books and my soap opera. That little television set was quite a companion.

After a full day at the pool, I rushed home to inhale the dinner you worked so hard to make. Then I raced out the door to meet my best friend Kevin at "the tramp," a neighbor's trampoline that we claimed as our own. Other kids joined us, but Kevin was all I really needed to make me happy. We bounced for hours, the lightening bugs sparkling all around us, illuminating our buoyant joy. As we got older, we played "spin the bottle" on that trampoline and cruised the neighborhood streets on the back of older kids' mopeds. It was like a dream, and we were always awakened too soon by the inevitability of autumn. On the first day of school, we'd protest at the bus stop by hiding up in a tree and throwing acorns at the bus below.

A storybook childhood...

Like yours, Mom.

I came from a working class family, but my friend Judy lived in a big white house that had a playhouse in the backyard. Her family had a maid...and they had potato chips and onion dip throughout the week— not just on Saturday nights! I liked staying over there for dinner. At our house, we ate a lot of my grandpa's vegetables. He was a vegetable farmer. The only thing I didn't like was rutabaga—that was bitter stuff and I didn't like how it made the house smell. At five o'clock, Mom put dinner on the table—usually pork chops or cottage ham, served with a vegetable, boiled potatoes, and rye bread and butter. Women weren't really creative with their cooking back then. There weren't any recipe books.

But there was time. Women took time to prepare meals for their families. There wasn't a rush to get food on the table. There was pride in the process. There was mindfulness before that was even a word.

You could taste the Love in every meal, in every bite. And my daddy made sure we ate every bite that was served to us.

Just like my dad… Being a member of his "Clean Plate Club" was non-negotiable most nights. Except when we had peas (which I once threw up on the table). Or when he was extra mellowed by his scotch and water. Then he let me off the hook.

Mom didn't like for Daddy to drink during the week. There were times, though, that Daddy would stop for a beer at a bar across the street from Ivorydale, the factory where he made soap for almost fifty years. There was no air conditioning in the factory and the temperatures sometimes rose to over a hundred degrees. But Daddy never complained. He would just get extra thirsty for a beer. Daddy would have loved to open a bar… Dick's Place, he would have called it. Mom knew that wouldn't have been a good idea.

Bars and family life don't mix well. Grandma always knew best.

Yes, she did. Other than throwing up peas, Nicki Beans, what else do you remember about our family dinners...over which I toiled?

You were the best cook, Mom! My childhood was full of casseroles. We thrived on chicken and Campbell's Soup or mayonnaise-based delicacies, topped with potato chips, cornflakes, or Chinese noodles. They were baked at 350 degrees for an hour and served steaming hot with rolls and applesauce…or a pineapple wedge dolloped with cottage cheese. If we were hungry between meals, we ate a slice of white bread with margarine. When we moved to Virginia, you discovered *Southern Living* magazine and expanded your recipe repertoire to include stir fry vegetables and rice, Cornish hens, and fancy desserts like Tapioca… But we always had a stash of Little Debbie treats for nights without finer desserts, right Mom?

You loved those oatmeal pies!

We ate at a perfectly set table at six o'clock when Dad, exasperated by the rush hour traffic, got home from his "long day at the office" selling Xerox copiers. He was still climbing that ladder. You held all of us around the dinner table, gently inquiring about Holly's day in the new territory of high school, answering Dad's countless questions about household matters, and responding with grace to my silly riddles.

"Hey Mom, how can a pocket be empty but still have something in it?" (Answer: it has a hole). "Get it, Mom? Hilarious, huh?"

It's no wonder I had so much indigestion.

•••

Tell us about your first dog, Mom.

*I realized my connection with animals when I was only two years old.
Aunt Sis gave me a puppy for my birthday. We named him Pepper. I
thought he was handsome, but I was the only one in the neighborhood
who did. My sister, Joy, said he was so ugly he was cute. To me, he was
everything. He ran the streets with the rest of the dogs, sometimes
bringing home a chicken from the farm up the street. That farmer was
not pleased. He took a shot at him a few times. Pepper was my best
friend. I dressed him in doll clothes and hats. I'd put him in the basket of
my bike and take him all around Winton Place with me. I must have been
a good rider because I don't remember any accidents—or maybe he was
a good jumper. He lived to be fourteen! Oh, that was a sad, sad day
when he died.*

We named my first childhood dog in honor of your Pepper. Dad brought
our Pepper home on Valentine's Day when I was just a toddler. He was a
beagle mix with kind eyes and droopy ears. He loved the warmth of a
fire and would lie dangerously close to our kerosene heater. Like you, I
had a fondness for dressing up my Pep in doll clothes. Over the years, he
developed a strong odor and some unsightly lumps and bumps, but we
loved him unconditionally, the same way you loved your Pepper. He
thrived on our affection for fourteen years, Mom. That was a sad, sad day
when he died.

*For your thirteenth birthday, a few years prior to Pep's passing, we got
our first golden retriever. What puppy love we had for Alex! Pep was a
little jealous, but I think Alex kept him moving in his final years.*

I was a late bloomer in many ways. I didn't outgrow playing dress-up
until well into puberty. For Alex's first Christmas, I painted her nose
with red fingernail polish and put antlers on her head. Pep watched me
with disapproval in his warty eyes. I think he might even have shaken his
head. The polish, obviously not meant for dog noses, chipped away
slowly, the remnants still visible in February. Clearly, I hadn't
considered the possible effects of this creative project.

*Clearly. Luckily, your error in judgement had no impact on Alex's
health. She filled our home with golden Love for fifteen years…*

Another sad, sad day when she passed…

A dog's Love is pure and effusive, a gift from Spirit. When a pet dies, the human heart breaks into a million pieces. Over time, it repairs itself…but the cracks remain forever. I suffered a lot of cracks in my lifetime.

•••

Let's talk about grandparents, Mom.

I adored my mom's parents, Grandma and Grandpa Parchman. Grandma called Grandpa "Hiney." He'd put his arm around her and she'd say, "You're so rough, Hiney." She was a little thing and he was a gentle giant, a big man with big hands. He was her protector. Mom encouraged me to walk by their house on my way to school, which was in the opposite direction. But those extra steps were worth it. They were always waiting for me, Grandpa on the front porch and Grandma waving from the window. Just a glimpse of me brought them such cheer.

Holly and I walked by their old house on our nostalgic visit to your childhood. We waved.

In elementary school, I came home for lunch everyday. Mom and I ate chicken noodle soup and cream cheese crackers on TV trays, while watching As the World Turns, *or as Grandpa called it, "The Turning World," on our black and white television set.*

Such simple pleasures in a turning world.

Once a year, Grandma took Joy and me to downtown Cincinnati. She was very slow and I'd get impatient. "Come on Grandma," I'd say. I was a little stinker! We'd shop and then go to a cafeteria where we'd fill up our trays with whatever our hearts desired. Traveling downtown was a big deal for Grandma—we had to take two or three buses! Every year on my sister's birthday, Grandma bought me a pencil with my name on it. She was so kind, but really self-conscious, perhaps a symptom of her unhappy childhood. Her mother was mean, but Grandma was just the opposite. Her sweetness showed up in her lemonade—the best lemonade ever! She squeezed her own lemons and was very liberal with the sugar. Grandma made sure we had plenty of fresh lemonade in the summertime.

Grandpa Parchman wanted to give us the moon. If Joy or I so much as picked up a leaf in the yard, he pulled out his wad of money and tucked a bill or two in our little fists. Grandpa always wore his farmer's overalls. But he could have worn a suit if he wanted—he had a brilliant mind for investments. When he died, he was a millionaire. No one knew it though. Mom said it was no one's business. Mom was Grandpa's Light.

As were you.

When Joy was contagious with diphtheria, I stayed with my grandparents for two weeks. All I wore was my red chenille robe. I spent a lot of time in the basement, sitting on a wooden box, helping Grandpa tie radishes to take to market.

Little Curly Top.

This home, my second home, was full of warmth. Whenever I walked through the door, Grandpa would say, "Go down in the basement and get yourself a pop." And when he was ready for me to go he'd say, "Here's your hat, what's your hurry?"

Daddy's parents were different. Their home was beautiful, but it didn't feel inviting to me. Grandma Schellinger had a distant kindness about her. From her kitchen window, she fed windmill cookies to a squirrel she named Jimmy. Her hair was wild and gray, and she pinned it up in a bun. Sometimes she wore a black hat and a veil over her face, masking her worried expression. As a child, I wondered if she was sad or afraid. I was just trying picture Grandma with a shag haircut, sporting a pair of sweatpants. That would have been a nice look for her. A nice life for her.

Grandpa Schellinger had sophisticated taste. He even made his own wine and goat cheese! On Thanksgiving he sliced the turkey with such precision that everything was cold by the time he finished. We ate cold turkey in a cold house. But I learned the art of presentation from Grandpa Schellinger. I enjoyed making things pretty, like the tuna fish sandwiches I served to Mom and Dad while they watched I Love Lucy. *I cut the sandwiches into little triangles and even removed the crusts. Mom appreciated my effort, but Daddy just threw the triangle in his mouth, his eyes never leaving the television set. Of course, I had to put a few chips on the side. No sandwich should ever be served without a little crunch to complement it!*

A very important life lesson.

I have the best memories of your parents, Mom. We'd burst through the doors on Galecrest Drive and Grandma would sing, "Who's comin'?" She greeted us with open arms, snuggling us in her soft bosom that smelled like cold cream mixed with a hint of rose oil. Grandpa, in his bare feet, was right behind her. "You're getting big, kid," he'd say, tousling my hair. There was almost always a ham in the oven...and German potato salad and a green Jello mold on the kitchen counter. The coffee table in the living room was never without a crystal bowl filled with starlight mints, remember Mom? I still love those fancy mints. To this day, I can taste my childhood in peppermint.

You would eat them like potato chips. I told you to suck on them. You never listened.

Grandpa taught Holly and me how to shoot pool in the musty basement with the red carpet. In between games, I'd pretend to be a bartender behind "Dick's Bar," while enjoying the smooth sounds of Engelbert Humperdinck on the radio. Grandpa finally got his bar…in his own basement. When he was ready for his can of beer in the garden, I'd go play cards with Grandma—31 was her game, and she was good. I think she let me win a lot. Grandpa never let me win at pool though.

During every visit, Grandma took me to Johnny's Toy Store, where I was allowed to pick out one stuffed animal. I felt bad for the ones I didn't pick. Then we'd go to a movie. It was always a feel-good kind of movie and Grandma would say, "What a nice story." After the movie, Grandpa would take us to the park to feed the ducks and ride the pedal boats. He did most of the pedaling. My grandparents were my angels on Earth before they were my angels in Heaven.

Two brilliant points on our star of 66.

My other grandparents were more formal. They were highly intelligent and eager to hear about my school projects and my plans for the future. Grandma passed on her passion for the written word to me, and for that, I will always be grateful. But our relationship was one of the mind, not of the heart.

Your grandmother endured some deep wounds throughout her life, including the sudden loss of her first husband, your dad's father, when Dad was just a baby. Her heart never fully mended. And so she built a wall around it... that we all experienced, in one way or another.

With Dad's parents, I was appreciated for my accomplishments. With your parents, Mom, I was cherished just for being me.

A child always knows the difference.

•••

How about your teenage years, Mom? I've seen the pictures. You were a beauty.

Those were the days of red lips and hot pants! Daddy would say, "Put some clothes on, kid... You're not going out of here in your undershirt!" Mom and Daddy loved having kids at our house. And my friends loved my parents. We had the best parties on Edgewood Avenue. Everyone showed up around eight o'clock for chips and dip and soda. Dad let the guys have beer sometimes. We pushed the kitchen table back and danced for hours to the light and happy songs of the day! After the guys left, Daddy went downtown to get cheeseburgers and fries for the girls. We put on our pajamas and just kept dancing! Such wonderful times. There was an innocence in my era that is lacking today.

I showed your grandchildren a video that your friend Alice made of one of your parties on Edgewood Avenue. They were amazed by the purity of the black and white scene of carefree teenagers dancing to silly songs...and Grandma and Grandpa beaming in the background.

We were living in the moment, long before that phrase became popular.

Frisch's Big Boy, a popular burger chain, was our hangout. We'd drive through the parking lot to see who was there. Just a couple cars made for a party. Someone would turn up their car radio and the girls would dance together, while the boys just stood back and watched us wiggle our booties. I had a lot of friends in high school, girls and guys. I had one serious boyfriend named Phil. He was very sexy and very complicated. I don't know why I was drawn to such complicated men in this life.

You certainly married one!

I did. Underneath your dad's charismatic image was a deep and abiding sensitivity. He did his best to keep it hidden, focussed instead on his pursuit of success...which included ensuring the happiness of you and your sister. He looked to me to lead the way in raising you girls.

85

He chose to take a blind eye to more than one of my teenage escapades and fashion statements. Some of my ensembles were less than family friendly. Remember that tie-dyed spandex mini-dress? And the bandannas I'd tie up my leg for extra punctuation?

Oh, I remember.

One early morning, after an all-night adventure, I snuck back into the house in that get-up and met Dad at the door. I told him I was out walking Pepper and Alex. "That's nice, honey," he said.

What he didn't know—or admit to knowing—couldn't hurt him. Like your grandmother, your dad protected his heart.

His tender heart...perhaps an exploration for another book, another time.

•••

Like you, Mom, I loved having parties our house...but most of them happened when you and Dad were out of town. Sorry, Mom. But we had a hot tub, a beer tap, and a yard full of trees where teenagers could do as they pleased. Our house was made for parties.

It was. Unfortunately, they had a spicier flavor than the parties I had as a teenager. I don't think there were any chips and dip and soda pops being served.

For my sixteenth birthday, you and Dad bought me a yellow Suzuki Samurai—my personalized plates touting my identity as a free spirit. I was...*THE WIND*. Of course, I couldn't drive my tiny truck during the three-month license suspension I got for speeding in the station wagon.

You only had your learners permit when you took the wagon out for that joy ride!

Not just a joy ride. I was actually being a good neighbor and citizen... Our friend, who had broken her arm, needed help with her baby. I was driving to her house to offer my assistance.

Sure, Nicki Beans.

Oh, but when I finally got behind the wheel of *THE WIND*, I was free! My friends would pile in and we'd head to the McDonalds parking lot to find out where the party was. Usually we'd end up in an office park or at a construction site, drinking beer bought with a fake ID, smoking menthol cigarettes, and listening to "Free Bird" on repeat.

You were a little full of yourself, Ms. Wind.

I was spoiled rotten. But you mothered me brilliantly throughout my childhood and adolescence, Mom. When I was little, you coached my cheerleading squad and made brownies for my Brownie troop. And as I grew into a terrible teenager, you gave me the perfect amount of space, allowing me to make mistakes... but intervening when I was in over my head.

Like when you became a pen pal with an inmate at the city jail?

Yeah, like then.

Well, I never let myself forget what it was like to be a teenager. I had some crazy times too, honey. Once, my friends and I squeezed into Alice Goldfarb's convertible and headed downtown to a burlesque show. We all wore trench coats. We looked so cool. But it was really dirty in there so we left just after arriving.

Mom! You rebel!

Back then, that was rebellious! I had a sheltered childhood, honey. When I graduated from high school, it seemed unlikely that I would go off to college. I was a girl, after all, and not the best student either. Plus, college was an expensive luxury for a working class family. But Mom could see how important it was to me so, as usual, she worked her magic with Daddy and convinced him to let me go to the University of Cincinnati for my associate's degree. I was over the moon! Daddy even taught me how to drive so I could get myself to and from campus. We'd go out for a lesson and I'd come home crying. He made me a nervous wreck! But I finally got my license and drove Daddy's blue Starfire to school everyday—I loved that car! I did a 360 in it on my way home once... Mom didn't tell Daddy about that.

You learned how to mother from the best. And so did I. Thank you for teaching her, Grandma. Thank you for teaching me, Mom.

The greatest pleasure of my life, honey.

•••

Because of you, Mom, family has always been the most important facet of my life.

As a child, you proclaimed your love for your dad and sister and me through countless gestures...the "Nicki cards," the framed poetry, the songs you wrote and recorded on cassette tapes. You loved big, honey.

Our unity as a foursome was an essential part of my identity and my sense of security.

You were happiest when we were all together.

One of the saddest days of my childhood was the day Holly left for college. I was twelve years old. Dad had packed up the old brown station wagon and we had all taken our assigned places in the car...Dad at the wheel, you beside him, and Holly and I in the back seat.

I can see us there.

There was that crevice in the back bench seat that separated the small part of the seat from the larger part. At the beginning of every long trip we took as a family, Holly would make me a deal. I could have the larger part of the bench if I promised not to cross over that crevice into "her space," as she called it. And I would agree to these conditions, but then sit as close to that crevice as possible without actually crossing over into her territory.

"Move over, Nicki," she'd plead, "you have the whole seat!"

"But I like it here," I'd say, making a bed for my stuffed dog in the extra space, "And besides, Henry needs to take a nap."

Holly would grit her teeth and roll her eyes, plugging herself into her Walkman and curling up as close to the window as she could get.

Then I'd irritate you and Dad until you, at your wits end, would give me a spoonful of allergy medicine.

You always sounded like you might be be catching a cold.

Sure, Mom. Whatever you need to tell yourself. Well, on this particular trip to Virginia Tech, Holly made the same back seat deal with me, but I decided to make a concerted effort to maintain the peace—and to avoid the decongestant stupor. I wanted to treasure these last few hours we had together as a foursome.

Oh Nicki, you are such a sentimental bean.

The Carpenters tape blaring from the car speakers was doing little to rally my spirits. Karen serenaded our family on many a road trip, didn't she, Mom?

Yes, and on this trip, she tugged hard at our heartstrings.

We tortured ourselves as we sang along with "Goodbye to Love" and "I Won't Last a Day without You." You wiped big tears from your cheeks, while Dad rambled on about "this great opportunity for Hol" and "time marching on."

In hindsight, he's the one who should have been getting the allergy medicine on our family road trips.

Oblivious to the emotional tension in the car, Holly continued tapping her knee to the REO Speedwagon pounding from her Walkman. She was beautiful with her wavy, dark hair and those big, brown eyes. She had flawless skin, and legs that seemed a mile long. In my prepubescent, awkward form, I looked to my sister for hope of what I might become. While jealousy reared its ugly head later, all I felt at that time was profound admiration. My sister commanded attention when she walked into a room. With the flash of a smile, she cast spells on anyone who crossed her path. Including me. How lucky was I to sit in this back seat with her! Even with six years and a crevice between us, I was still Holly Rhode's sister. And that was all that mattered.

When I was born, Holly was skeptical about the idea of a new baby in the house. But later, she confessed that she fell in love with me the first time I grabbed her pinky finger. Her Pepto Bismol habit began when I cracked my head open at nine months old, then burned my hand when I was three, and in her care.

She couldn't bear to see you in pain! The Pepto soothed her stomach, but not her soul.

89

In pictures, we looked like typical sisters of the seventies. I loved hamming it up in front of the camera, adorable as I was in my plaid leisure suit. Unfortunately, Holly, who you dressed to match me, was not as cute in geometric fashion. Bless her heart, at age ten, she was not the specimen of beauty that she is today.

That was the style, honey. But you're right, it was not her best look.

In one of my most treasured pictures of my sister, she is decked out in her ballerina leotard, pot belly hanging over her tutu, tiara adorning her head, a toothy grin radiating from her pudgy face. Even then I thought she was the most perfect creature in the world, and I wanted to be just like her. I emulated her in every way possible... from the way she walked and talked to her ever-changing array of favorites...

"What's your favorite color now, Hol?" I'd ask.

"I'm not telling you," she'd say.

"Is it still green? It was green last week. I like green. Do you?"

You drove her crazy!

I even tried to copy her lazy tongue. Poor Holly had a hard time keeping her tongue in her mouth, so she had to do daily exercises that would help strengthen that muscle. Remember, Mom?

Of course... That was the quietest time of my day!

Well, as strange as it may seem, I thought her lazy tongue was worth imitating, so I walked around with my tongue hanging out of my mouth too.

For better or worse, you idolized your sister.

As we got older, one of my hobbies was embarrassing Holly in front of her boyfriends. And she had a lot of boyfriends! I made a habit of gathering information to leverage at critical times. It was less about power and more about getting her attention. Once, I interrupted her make-out session on the orange and brown plaid sofa to tell her boyfriend that she was on her period.

Nicki, you were a little devil.

Despite my irritating ways, my sister tolerated and indulged me. From the time I can remember, "family nights," as I coined them, were the highlight of my week. Every Friday, I begged Holly to forget about her high school party and stay home with us. I made the idea as appealing as possible, reminding her of the popcorn and the tickle fights and *The Love Boat* episode she just couldn't miss. She succumbed to my shameless pleading about one Friday night a month. We snuggled up in our flannel pajamas next to the fireplace with our old beagle, Pepper. I can still hear the popcorn popping in the old fashioned machine as Holly and I predicted how the stories on this particular Love Boat cruise would unfold.

A storybook scene...but it was time to turn the page.

•••

When we finally arrived at Virginia Tech, Dad parked the car and Holly reached for the door handle. I grabbed her hand and implored her to stay. She offered me a quick and confident smile as she opened the door, the wings she'd been hiding under her Coca Cola t-shirt bursting forth and opening wide. Frozen in awe, all I could do was witness my sister's launch from the nest of our station wagon.

With heavy boxes and bags, and even heavier hearts, we followed Holly through the hallways of her dormitory. The chaos of activity distracted me from my sadness long enough to appreciate the excitement of this new beginning for my newly-winged bird, my Virginia Tech Hokie.

Dad assembled the loft, while we unpacked pieces of home. So Holly wouldn't forget.

I stared at the framed photo of the four of us, all laughing, on the day of Holly's senior prom. We hosted the dinner that evening and you insisted on being the waitress.

I took my job very seriously. I had nametag and a notepad to take orders. Did I wear a hairnet?

You had quite a flare for the dramatic...

...and a yearning for my sister's affection.

While you continued to unpack, I went to look for Holly, who was lost, perhaps intentionally, in the tornado of move-in day. I glared at a parade of pretty girls in matching pink t-shirts, holding signs advertising their sorority, their lifelong sisterhood. When I found Holly, who was also watching this spectacle, I reminded her that she already had a sister. She didn't need any more. Again, she offered a quick and confident smile, but this time she didn't fly away. She hugged me. As if I was the only girl that mattered. The only sister she'd ever need.

Years later, Holly gave me a birds nest necklace—two freshwater pearls, the eggs that were us, wrapped in wire. It brought me back to that day in her dormitory.

A treasure of sisterhood.

When Dad finished putting the loft together, he announced it was time to go. You and Holly embraced for what seemed like an eternity, and I looked on, unable to breathe through my tears.

The three of us, a beautiful mess.

Bewildered and perhaps unsettled by our profuse expression of emotion, Dad hurried us along to the car. It was a silent journey home, save for some random sniffles. Dad rested his hand on your knee as you stared out the window. And I sat where Holly had, a new view of a world without her beside me guarding the crevice.

When we got home, I went straight to her room. I wanted to smell her signature scent of drugstore perfume. After that, I kept her door closed so that I could pretend she was still behind it.

The first year was the hardest. We would cry anytime someone asked about Holly and especially when a sad song came on the radio. Chicago was our muse of melancholy then, and we were brought to our knees with "Hard Habit to Break." Remember, Mom?

> *"Now being without you*
> *Takes a lot of getting used to*
> *Should learn to live with it*
> *But I don't want to..."*

I would come home from school and find you sweeping out the garage, radio blaring, tears streaming...

We would just fall into each other.

Sweeping and weeping...

•••

We counted the days between Holly's homecomings. Holidays, or "Hollydays," as I cleverly called them, were extra special. Dad started playing *The Carpenter's Christmas Collection* at Thanksgiving. And you poured over your *Southern Living* recipes, seeking the finest cuisine for Holly's time at home.

But it was the creamy comfort of my everyday chicken casserole that she craved. Even the most familiar foods tasted better when we were all together.

After a couple years of harassing Holly to come home every weekend, using your Chicken Divan as incentive, I began to consider that there might be life outside of family nights with Captain Stubing and Julie McCoy.

Your adolescence arrived like a flash flood, honey. Overnight, you transformed from an awkward little girl, with buck teeth and a goofy giggle, who made up voices for her stuffed animals...to a young woman in tight jeans and makeup, who sang Madonna's "Like a Virgin" like a prayer.

But my family remained the core of my world, Mom.

That never changed.

When I was fifteen and Holly was almost twenty-one, we took a family spring break trip to Florida. I'm not sure what you and Dad were thinking, or if you were thinking, but you let us stay in our own condominium, across the street from yours.

Obviously, we weren't thinking.

For the first time ever, we transcended the big sister and little sister paradigm and became best friends. Decked out in our short skirts with our big hair, we hitchhiked to Fort Lauderdale, drank ourselves silly, and caught the attention of two professional tennis players. Holly stopped being my friend and started being my big sister again when I disappeared on the beach with my tennis player, quite innocently, of course. Turns out she didn't like the fact that her little sister was growing up, and secretly, I liked the way she looked out for me.

I liked that too, honey.

Let's sing some Madonna, Mom…

Oh, Nicki Beans!

•••

We had charmed childhoods, both of us. But there were truths underneath this truth. There was fear and longing underneath this joy. Stories have layers, and each layer deserves to be acknowledged for what it brings to the whole.

I think it's time we do some spring cleaning of our lives. Not just dusting off the top layer, but honoring and digging deep into this life and all the lives that still echo within us…

…because this one little life is just a fraction of our existence. Not only are there other stories within this lifetime's storybook, but there are volumes and volumes of storybooks that illuminate our soul's evolution from the beginning of time…or no-time.

Life is but a series of dreams…

I had a dream recently, Mom, that felt like a message for this book.

Our dreams can be our greatest teachers…

We were in the station wagon—you, me, and Grace.

My Grace, my first grandbaby, my grace.

You were in the front seat. I was in the middle seat. Grace was in the way back. And I was driving, the steering wheel in my hands—in the middle seat! My view of the narrow and winding mountain road was limited, at best. I was exhilarated and horrified at once. In a cold sweat, I awoke with your words on my heart.

Be bold and courageous on this this wild ride through the stories of our lives. But give Spirit the wheel...

...because I can't see it all.

This book is your vehicle to Truth, honey. But you are carrying many precious passengers who are viewing the dream of this life through their own conditioned lenses, experiencing their own relative truths.

Human truth is a matter of perspective.

Everyone is a unique manifestation of Spirit. We keep coming back to this setting called Earth, assuming different roles with different challenges, so that we continue to learn and grow.

Until we wake up from the dream and remember that we are infinite beings, a part of the whole and the whole itself.

In my current state of formless reality, without a distinct body or a singular perspective, the boundless Light of my essence is so clear.

The challenge is to abide in the awareness of our Light while on Earth, while trapped in the illusion of separation and the drama of this one little dream.

To be in a body is a gift, Nicki Beans. The magic and miracle of the human experience is thrilling!

There is a fine line between thrill and fear.

Dissolving that line is your work, honey. And taking this wild ride with Spirit is part of it. The destination is already within you... you just have to wake up and remember it.

•••

I didn't want to come back to Earth this time around, Mom. I didn't want to be contained in a body again, to be consumed by the illusion. I didn't want to risk the corruption of my Light.

And Spirit assured you that this was to be a lifetime of healing.

So I agreed to come back with one big condition.

That I would be your mom.

We've traveled together through many lifetimes, you and I.

And we've made many soul contracts in no-time. Agreements to teach and learn from each other, to help each other remember our Divinity while on Earth.

It took awhile for me to make the leap into your belly.

You certainly took your sweet time. But you were worth the wait.

I came in with a lot of fear.

And an insatiable need for assurance and connection.

I wore you out, huh, Mom?

I knew I would never be able to fill all of your emotional needs.

Breastfeeding would have been a good start.

Oh, Nicki Beans. Here we go again with the breastfeeding. It was the seventies and I was not a hippie mama. Breastfeeding was not in vogue in my suburban circle.

I know, Mom. I don't blame you for that. If Mother Mary herself had nursed me twenty-four hours a day, I still would have cried out for more.

You were a source of intense longing and undulating emotions. I had to meet you with firm boundaries.

You gave me structure and stability. You kept me safe in a world that felt dangerous.

That structure and stability, that logical kind of love, was for my own safety too. Your sensitivity overwhelmed me. There were other family dynamics at play that required my attention as well. I had to conserve my energy, to ensure that everyone received what they needed from me.

Another dream, a dream of my childhood, landed abruptly on my heart last night.

Dad built me a throne. I didn't ask for it, but I didn't deny it either. It was made of wood, a tree's sacrifice. You were there, planted firmly in the gravel driveway, hard white blossoms falling from your limbs, as if somehow you were the tree that was sacrificed for Dad's effort. You looked at me on my throne and smiled, but it was Holly you took in your arms. "You are my baby girl," you said aloud to her.

Your dad loved you both, but he had an ease with you. You two had a playful banter, as well as a comfortable silence together. But with Holly, there was often friction. And I was the protector of her heart.

I was blissfully unaware of these dynamics as a child…or maybe I enjoyed being the crowned one and chose not to look too closely at our family alliances. This would be a story that would evolve through the summer, fall, and winter of your life, Mom. And it's a story that still vibrates for Dad and Holly and me today. But in the springtime of my life, I only remember laughing with my dad and worshipping my sister.

You and your sister were separated by six years and vastly different soul needs…but I made it a priority to secure your closeness, your appreciation for one another.

You made sure we knew that sisterhood was a gift.

The greatest gift. You will know each other longer and more intimately than you will know anyone else in this lifetime.

I know, Mom. I won't forget.

•••

In my family, I was also the youngest of two girls. But my relationship with my sister was different. Our family dynamic was different.

It was a very different time.

My daddy really wanted a boy. "Cheese and crackers," he said when I was born, "another damn girl, how about that?" Somehow I knew, coming into this lifetime, that I had better be tough. I knew Daddy loved me, but it wasn't a warm and easy kind of love.

You got your warm and easy love from your mom and grandparents.

This is true. But outside of happiness, there wasn't a lot of tolerance for emotional expression in my family. In the face of any disturbance, Grandma would respond, "It'll be fine... Just smile and be nice." This worked for her, but not always for me.

A happy presentation was most important, regardless of the feelings behind the smile.

And I had a lot of feelings I just couldn't contain. As a small child, I was a biter and a pincher. I once told Grandpa Schellinger to shut up. He was mean and he scared me, but I had a sense, even as a child, that he should be put in his place.

Whatever the consequences, you let people know what was on your mind.

I certainly sucked on my share of Ivory soap bars!

Disrespecting your elders called for big punishment.

It didn't matter that the elder was undeserving of respect. Sucking on the soap my daddy made with his own hands was worth the crime of disrespecting his father. Grandpa Schellinger owned his own hardware store. He was a member of fancy clubs and he had fancy hobbies. He did very well for himself, but he did very little for his three children. When my aunt's husband was laid off from work, my daddy quit high school so that he could work full-time for the family. He had a deeply ingrained work ethic, and he gave money to his sister every week for a long time. When my grandparents died, the only thing they left Daddy was a bar shaker. The rest of their belongings went to his brother and sister. I didn't know why. Maybe I wasn't supposed to know.

My grandpa was the strongest man I ever knew.

On the outside, honey. But there was a broken little boy behind that tenacious temperament.

People didn't talk about family dysfunction back then, did they, Mom? It was just accepted and absorbed in the genetic code, to appear later as disease.

Yes, it was…and yes, it did.

•••

My sister was much sweeter than me. She liked being by herself. She'd go to her room and put music on her record player, and we wouldn't see her for hours. She seemed so content with life. In pictures of her as a child, she looked dreamy, even celestial. She was thirteen years old when she was diagnosed with rheumatoid arthritis. Her joints ached and her body tired easily. She spent more and more time in her room with her records playing behind her closed door. I wondered if she was sad. Or still content.

You wished for more of a connection with your sister.

I don't think we really understood each other. I was the opposite of content. I wanted to make noise! That's probably why I liked tap dancing so much. Hop up, back hop down, shuffle side to side, kick step, kick step.

Little dancing diva!

I think Daddy liked my lively nature, even though he didn't show me a lot of affection. He had a harder time with Joy's quiet demeanor. Sometimes the anger Daddy harboured from his childhood escaped…and landed on my sister. Theirs was a challenging dynamic, but Mom could quell any conflict with her kindness.

The simple goodness of Grandma's presence could diminish any disruption…temporarily.

But, like Daddy, I had some fire in me. I wanted to be disrupted…and disruptive. This seemed impossible to reconcile with my mom's incessant call to be good, do good, and make life good for others. Plus, for much of my childhood, the unspoken pain of my daddy's wounds and my sister's illness permeated the house. The anger and sadness around these circumstances allowed no room for other big emotions. So as I got older, I tried not to make a lot of noise. I tried.

Were there feelings you denied to keep the peace?

I had a hard time in school. While never diagnosed, I'm sure I had some learning disabilities. The classroom wasn't a safe place for me. I felt shame around my inability to grasp information...and my confidence was compromised. I didn't have the words to express my feelings then, and even if the words had been available, I probably wouldn't have shared them. Given what Joy had to endure, it would have been selfish. On the outside, everything looked just right for me. I was pretty and healthy and I had lots of friends. But on the inside, there was a desire to be more, a voice that was struggling to be heard.

Without the tools or the opportunity to explore your inner landscape, you ignored your longing and navigated life from the outer layer of appearance.

There is radiant authenticity in our ancestral line. But we also carry an artificial light in our DNA. Masters of optimism, we've been coded with the ability to deny the shadows of our stories.

This code was a means of survival in many cases. There were women in our family history whose lives depended on their ability to hide their pain.

Hidden pain is always found, eventually.

In a healing session, I was shown a scene from the life of one of our ancestors, Mom. It was hard to see.

You were ready to see it, honey.

The woman looked like you, elegant and alluring. She was in an arranged marriage with a dark and sexually sadistic man. Her luster fueled his aggression and his desire to conquer her. She was trapped during a time when women did not share the reality of their abuse. She had no choice but to pretend and project an artificial light so that no one would ever know the magnitude of her pain.

This pattern was handed down from generation to generation, locked in our cellular memory. The hardships changed, but the response to them remained the same. "It'll be fine... Just smile and be nice." Someone would have to break the cycle.

That someone was you.

•••

I was in my fifties when I allowed myself to admit that my mom's perspective on Life had flaws.

In one enlightened moment of rage, you found your voice: "I'm tired of being nice! Nice is way overrated!"

I don't know why I was angry, just that I was, and I no longer had the energy to conceal it.

It wasn't that you didn't express heightened emotion prior to that. You'd cry when you were sad and yell when you were mad. But those episodes were brief, and sometimes explosive, as if you had to hurry the emotion's visit before the smile's eminent return. It confused me as a child when, in the midst of a furious rant about my messy room, you'd answer the phone with the cheeriest of greetings. "Where did the anger go…" I wondered.

It was hiding in the shadows…

Unlike the story of our ancestor, my life, this time around, contained no major trauma. But emotion cannot be measured or compared. The heart does not judge the story creating the anger or sadness or fear. It just feels what it feels. And when we do not allow our feelings to speak, we neglect the very essence of our humanity. Over this lifetime, I began to see the Truth of the artificial light I sometimes shed on the world. Yet I had grown comfortable with that light, so I had no motivation to turn it off. It was my illness that broke this pattern in me. Cancer gave me no choice but to rest in my truest self, to surrender to the natural Light of my being—the Light that needs no effort to shine.

It was the greatest gift you ever gave to Holly and me…and to everyone who crossed your path.

While I was no longer hiding my shadow, I continued to value my privacy. Being intimate with my pain didn't mean I needed to share it with others. Maintaining my autonomy, as much as I could in my final season, remained an essential part of my character.

This self-reliance didn't come through in my DNA, at least not in my relationship with you.

As a young mother, I wasn't conscious of the family values that were guiding my interface with the world. So when you came in with your raw and open fear, I was overwhelmed.

It was part of our soul pact to spare you none of my inner turbulence. Over many lifetimes, you had cultivated the energy of the archetypal healer. As I allowed the pain of my expansive existence to emerge, I needed you like I needed air.

Your vulnerability was a stark contrast to what I had known in this life. It was liberating...and terrifying. I worried it would destroy you—and perhaps me too. So I did what I knew how to do. I met your primal cry with a forced light. I said it would all be fine. And I told you to smile.

And I did. I smiled a lot, Mom. But I also carried the guilt and shame of lifetimes like a security blanket. I was attached to the suffering I felt I deserved. My need for atonement was visceral in my incessant questions, "Did I hurt you? Are you mad at me? Do you still love me?"

You were sorry for everything. You couldn't bear the thought of causing harm to anyone or anything. You needed constant affirmation that no one was angry or upset with you in any way. Affirmation that you were a good little girl.

The natural curiosity I had about my body caused me to doubt my goodness. I was debilitated by the fear of being impure.

You had so much sexual shame, and no basis for it...in this lifetime.

I felt particularly charged at church. At the end of each service, the minister would call to the front those who needed Jesus to wash away their sins.

And you would get this look in your eye like your life depended on being forgiven. I would assure you that you had done nothing wrong, but you didn't believe me.

It wasn't true. I had perpetrated wrongs in many lifetimes past. And several of those experiences were related to the church. And to sex. While I could feel those memories as a child, I couldn't see them until much later in my adult life. But they were alive in my karmic body and as real to me as what happened the day before.

At the time, I attributed your odd obsessions to an overactive imagination and a profound sensitivity. Certainly, this was just a phase that you would outgrow, I reasoned.

In the face of fear, my only recourse, as I could see it, was to be nice. Really nice. To be good and do good and make life good for others.

Like Grandma.

To be good was to be loved. To be loved was to be safe. Eventually, my quest for goodness intersected with my drive for perfection. Eraser marks on my homework or a blemish on my skin was unacceptable. Behind my smile, I was tormented by my fear of being imperfect and *bad...* in a dangerous world.

But your world wasn't dangerous. In your storybook childhood, your fear made no sense to me. Years later, I would see the bigger picture of your struggle—the past life scars that needed to be explored and redefined as holy moments in your soul's evolution. At the time, I didn't understand. I'm sorry, honey.

While I navigated the world with perfection and goodness as my guides, you walked right beside me, Mom. With you, I always knew that I was good and loved... and safe.

A promise I made to you in no-time.

My teenage years were a welcome distraction from my suffering. I willed my fear into hiding and allowed the drama of adolescence and the importance of my identity to command my thoughts and feelings through high school.

In adolescence, we spend our energy building and maintaining the egoic identity. Over time, we can see this identity for the illusion that it is and the false sense of safety it provides. But in the springtime of life, we embrace the dream of being alive in our unique and pretty forms, blissfully unaware of the work we are destined to do later.

I have to remember this with my own kids, Mom. I find myself pushing them to look within, dig for meaning, discover the lessons.

Let them enjoy their springtime, honey. Because at some point, every one of us must acknowledge and tend to our pain…before we can be freed from it.

···

My real work began in college.

It didn't surprise me that you wanted to pursue an education in social work. While you had a lot of fun in high school, you also developed a strong identity around helping others and saving the world.

And, with the upbringing I had, my world was very small, very savable. But moving to the city opened my eyes to the overwhelming volume of suffering that existed…

…triggering those old cellular memories of guilt and shame.

They were all-consuming, and I didn't have the capacity to hold my suffering and the suffering I encountered all around me. So they merged. And I obsessed—could the danger I feared in the world be inside of me?

You convinced yourself that you were at fault for the world's darkness. That you were an imposter of Light.

To compensate, I was *really good*. I signed up for every volunteer opportunity available. I maintained a perfect grade point average. I won awards and scholarships. And the respect of many.

You discovered the artificial light in your genetic code, and you cast it wide.

It worked for a while. The validation I received from others muted my loathing within.

But it wasn't sustainable—nothing artificial or external is. Your relentless pursuit of perfection and goodness was not only a manifestation of your ancestral and karmic blueprints, but also a symptom of a medical condition.

Obsessive compulsive disorder—an extra sticky brain chemistry that prevents any thought from simply crossing the mind. I was certain that every thought I had contained a message for me. And many of the messages were of catastrophic proportions. Supporting the guilt and shame with which I came into this lifetime. Supporting my addiction to suffering and my search for a story I believed would set me free.

Things got a little crazy. Medication seemed the only answer.

It saved me at the time, Mom. As did you and your firm boundaries. You realized that your reassurance was only perpetuating my compulsive tendencies and leading me further into the delusions of my sticky brain.

Denying you the comfort you craved broke my heart, but I knew it was a necessary part of your journey back to yourself, back to the Truth of your innate human goodness and your Divine perfection.

It would be a slow journey, on which I was often paralyzed by *bad* thoughts and an insatiable need for answers I would never find. In the dangerous landscape of my mind, I was not safe.

But you were loved.

Your Love was the only thing I never doubted.

I just wanted you to be happy.

I wanted that too, Mom. So, with your Love and my little yellow pills, I put my fear to sleep. And I started living again...

•••

Summer

···

Now we find ourselves in the full bloom of summer. Can you feel the vitality of the season, Mom?

I can feel the heat! Let's sit under Oakley. Thank you for your shade, dear tree. Some lemonade sure would be nice…with extra sugar like my grandma used to make. Ah, and here it is—manifestation is so easy in Heaven! And on Earth too, when humans open their eyes and hearts and minds to what is possible!

We have the innate power to co-create with the Universe. What else might be possible?

Chocolate chip cookies, still warm from the oven!

Delicious! I used to love baking cookies with you, Mom.

You'd eat all the dough, Nicki Beans, and we'd hardly have any cookies left to bake!

Oh, the dough! The sweetest indulgence…

…the best stuff of Life.

Let's lean into the fire of summer, Mom. From its blaze comes our passion, our fullness, our force. In this creative time, we long to be seen and valued for what we contribute to world. We expand our definition of family, home, and work as we discover the magnitude of our potential, the power of our dreams. Fully absorbed by the illusion of life and our limited perspective on being human, we strengthen our identities and cultivate our unique gifts.

So focused on what's next for our little self, we often forget the magic of the moment and the vastness of who we really are.

We are busy. There is little rest in the summer of our lives. Even at night, a frenetic and wild energy abounds, something always stirring within and around us.

Ripe with beauty, we fall in love with the world...and with our destined one.

Yes. Love. In the summer of our lives, we fall in love. That's the best part of summer, Mom. Tell us about how you met Dad.

This is a nice story.

You sound like Grandma.

Well, it's true, Nicki Beans. There's not a lot of drama in my storybook this time around. Nothing shocking. Some might find this memoir boring, perhaps not worthy of reading.

What do you think?

I think every soul story is fascinating. Every life is an integral piece of the whole. There are those who might argue that we only learn from suffering and longing. I happen to think we learn a lot from happiness and contentment too. All of Life is exhilarating when we fully immerse ourselves in it.

And when we shine authentic Light on it.

We are breaking the pattern of artificial light, honey. We are honoring the layers of truth as we tell the whole of our stories. But sometimes, across the countless stories in every lifetime, the happy ending is the

Truth. Your aspiration for purity is worthy, but not at the expense of Life's joy. Embrace the joy, Nicki Beans...and be grateful for the happy endings.

...

I hear you, Mom. And I am grateful...because one of the happy endings in your storybook this time around was me. And it began with Dad, on a warm spring evening in 1964.

I was in my second year at the University of Cincinnati. It was a Friday so, naturally, I was getting ready for a date.

Did you ever *not* have a date, Mom?

Rarely. Much to my daddy's chagrin, there was almost always a boy on my doorstep. I was a social butterfly, honey. I had a lot of fun...in a nice girl kind of way, of course.

Of course.

On that particular night, my friend Bonnie was out cruising the city with a boy named Owen and his fraternity brother Bill Rhode.

My dad!

Your father was looking for a date, and Bonnie suggested they stop by my house. When they arrived, I came downstairs in my bathrobe, with curlers in my hair.

You didn't!

I did. Don't be cute, Nicki Beans. Now, like I said, I already had a date for the evening, so I had to decline your father's invitation.

He was crushed.

Evidently, because he called the next day and the day after that and the day after that...until I agreed to go out with him the next weekend.

Did you like him immediately?

I thought he was interesting. He had a sophisticated sense of fashion. When he picked me up, he was wearing a fedora. I wore a cranberry colored dress—it was sleeveless with a V-neck. I chose flat shoes for the evening because I thought your dad was short! Imagine my surprise when all six feet and one inch of him showed up at my door...

I love this story!

We went to see The Sound of Music *and we held hands. Afterwards, we went to a local college bar and your dad introduced me to cognac.*

Very refined.

Everyone at school thought your dad was wealthy. He had a convertible and a scooter that he drove around campus, which caught the attention of many pretty coeds, I'm sure. He had a boat too...but he wasn't wealthy. He just worked hard and spent all his money on toys!

Were you smitten?

Indeed, I was. Word spread quickly around campus that Nancy and Bill were off the market. Your dad became a permanent fixture in my house. Sometimes my daddy let him stay the night in the basement. But he locked the door, a clear message that there was to be no "funny business" under his roof.

How long did you date before you got engaged?

It was less than a year. In a testament of his love for me, your dad traded his scooter and his boat for a diamond. He attached it to a travel brochure of honeymoon possibilities and threw it to me across my parents' living room.

Did you have any doubts?

None. I could see my future with this man. We got married on my parents' wedding anniversary, a day that promised blessings. I had a beautiful gown, fitted and simple. We left right after the reception for a honeymoon in Indiana.

A honeymoon in Indiana?

We stayed at a nice resort. Your dad had just gotten a job at Xerox, and we only had time for a long weekend away. It was…nice.

Nice. We love that word.

Oh, Nicki Beans!

•••

As newlyweds, our life was charmed. We had our day jobs, our college friends, and a cute little apartment on Westwood Northern Boulevard. But outside of our insulated existence, the Vietnam War was brewing, and it was only a matter of time before Dad's draft number would be called.

That must have been scary, Mom.

We knew that if Dad were drafted, his return from Vietnam would be less than likely. So he decided to enlist voluntarily with the Army's Medical Service Corps, which meant a three-year active commitment to the military.

In wartime.

It was our best option. And there was no question that the next step was to start our family. I couldn't bear the thought of being alone while your dad was away…and all I ever wanted to be was a mother. Unlike you, Holly was conceived quickly, just before Dad left for basic training camp in Texas.

A blessing.

Shortly before our first wedding anniversary, Dad came home from basic training to a very pregnant wife and military orders to report to Fort Benning, Georgia.

What was that like, knowing you'd be having your baby in a strange place, away from the only home you'd ever known, away from your mom?

It was hard, but being pregnant was a Divine distraction. It was like having a secret inside of me, something to protect.

You loved us so perfectly…even before we were born.

That was easy. Loading up the convertible Mustang with all of my clothes was not. I was not about to leave my style in Cincinnati.

Of course not. Georgia was in desperate need of a peach like you!

There were a lot of tears on our trip down south. And it was lonely on the army base. But I stayed positive by keeping our home neat and clean, and focusing on the little Life inside of me. I spent our meager budget and my limited energy on meals. Yet there never seemed to be enough food to satisfy Dad's appetite. Our weekly splurge at the Dairy Queen buoyed us. What a treat that was!

Simple pleasures.

Your sister made her grand entrance into the world on November 23, 1966…

…and you miraculously lived to tell about it.

Military doctors were not known for their bedside manner in those days. And at twenty-two years old, I knew nothing about giving birth and even less about advocating for myself. I labored for twenty-three hours, enduring pain, exhaustion, and the doctor's incessant commentary about my "inadequate pelvis." He tried forceps and other inhumane instruments to forcefully bring your sister into the world, futile efforts that only caused more trauma.

That's awful, Mom. Where was Dad?

It was against military protocol to allow men into the delivery room. But in the twenty-fourth hour, the doctor made an exception. My distress was potent and it was clear, even to this idiot doctor, that I needed my husband. Dad's warm eyes calmed me and perhaps had the same effect on the doctor, who finally decided to perform a cesarean section…

A call that should have been made hours earlier!

In the end, I had your sister in my arms, and that was all that mattered. Fittingly, it was the day before Thanksgiving. I was grateful beyond words, despite the fact that the doctor forgot to order me a meal before he left for his holiday.

You were high on Love, Mom.

Your sister and I have shared many lifetimes as warriors. This was a different kind of battle, but it was fought with the same champion spirit. Our souls know how to survive against all odds...together.

This was obvious, from her birth to your death. You two shared a tenacity that I could only admire. What would trigger me to retreat would inspire you to rise. Your power was reflected in different ways—your earthy presence subtler than Holly's fire—but the energy behind this power was born of the same passion to defend and uphold Love. As Holly's mom, you were her ultimate protector...and in your illness, she became yours.

Full circle.

•••

Let's get back to the beginning...

One of my most cherished memories occurred a month after Holly was born. I couldn't imagine spending her first Christmas on the army base, so Dad loaded up the Mustang again—this time with baby paraphernalia—and off we drove through the snow, home for the holidays.

I can just see you walking through those doors on Galecrest Drive and into your parents' waiting arms.

There were few times, across all my lifetimes, that I felt so much joy.

There is nothing quite like sharing your child with your parents for the first time. It's the ultimate, "Look what I did, Mom," coupled with a hallowed reception into the sacred and shared territory of parenthood. That roaring and unspoken confirmation in the smiles of new grandparents, "Yeah, look what you did, kid."

A year later, Dad left for his tour of duty in Vietnam, and Holly and I came home to Galecrest Drive. Mom and Daddy were wonderful support, but I lived in constant fear for your dad's life. I got letters almost daily, as well as weekly audio tapes. Your dad was quite a romantic...and quite a planner. In between his oaths of eternal devotion, he'd share his architectural visions for our first home. He couldn't wait to get back to our life together.

I'm so glad you saved his letters and tapes. They reflect such innocence, such hope...

...such Love.

•••

It was a blessing in disguise that Holly was a challenging toddler. She kept me busy and distracted from my own suffering. I called her my little devil. She must have broken a half dozen pairs of my sunglasses that year, looking me in the eye as she crushed them in her little fists. My defiant child monster!

How did Grandma and Grandpa cope with Holly's behavior?

Oh, they just smiled. They loved her, they loved us—unconditionally. But we were a disruption to their lives. I tried to stay out of their way as much as possible. That wasn't easy with a child like Holly. It seemed as if she were everywhere at once. I couldn't keep up with her.

Good thing she was cute! There's a precious picture of her sitting on her little potty, beside Grandpa in his recliner...watching a rerun of *I Love Lucy*, watching Love unfold around her.

One of the few times she was still!

After a turbulent year on our own, your sister and I went to the airport to bring your dad home. I was worried that she wouldn't remember him, that she wouldn't go to him. As the soldiers piled off the plane, Holly called each of them "DaDa," but it was your father for whom she reached. In the embrace of our reunion, I exhaled...completely.

How was the transition for Dad?

There was certainly a period of adjustment. In the middle of the night, he would mistake thunderstorms for gunfire and fall to the floor in sheer panic. But he never wanted to talk about his experience in Vietnam. When I asked questions, he changed the subject, eager to get back to this reality—our family, our home, his career…and most importantly, our plans. The future was his focus. What he repressed I may never know.

And then I came along…

…to complete our family.

•••

Your turn, Nicki Beans. Tell us your love story, the story of you and Mike.

Well, we might need to rewind a bit to the springtime of my life…when I met my prince.

Enter the romantic storyteller!

Just sit back and listen, Mama…

Once upon a time, not very long ago, there lived a prince. And like all the girls at Monacan High School, I admired him from afar. He was a typical teenage heartthrob—a cool confidence combined with a very appealing physique, piercing blue eyes, sun-kissed skin, and sandy brown hair with little ringlets that fell perfectly on the back of his neck. He was the star of the varsity football team. Watching him run out of the locker room every Friday night in those tight little football pants gave all the girls a thrill…

Oh, Nicki!

The prince came into my life on the first day of my sophomore year. I strolled into my third period honors calculus class, and there he was, sitting in the back row, drumming a brand new pencil on the desk. Our eyes met for a moment, and he acknowledged me with a head nod. I managed an awkward smile, and with weak knees, collapsed into the first desk on my path. I was blushing fiercely.

You are still a blusher!

Then the teacher, Mrs. Ragsdale, made an announcement that would change my life forever.

"Class," she said, "before we begin, I will be seating you alphabetically. This will be your assigned seat for the rest of the year." Well, my hands began to sweat profusely and the blood of my whole body rushed to my ears. For you see, the prince was a "P" and I was an "R." And there was no "Q" in this particular class!

Gasp!

Names were called and students scrambled around the room to take their seats…until finally, my monumental moment arrived. In my recollection, the room was silent and in slow motion, a spotlight on the prince and me, as Mrs. Ragsdale read our names off her roll. I stood on wobbly legs to find my way across the room to the desk that would hold my destiny. When I arrived an eternity later, all I could do was stare at that perfect head in front of me, those precious little curls at the base of that kissable neck. I wondered how in the world I would ever learn anything about math sitting behind this beautiful boy!

Oh, please!

Then he reached behind him with a folded note in his hand. My heart sank as I took it, carefully, so as not to touch his fingers. That would certainly have sent me over the edge and into teenage hysteria. Nonchalantly, I tucked the note into my calculus textbook and tried to focus on Mrs. Ragsdale's mathematical meanderings…until I couldn't stand it any longer. I unfolded the paper as if I were unfolding my fate and read, "Do you have any gum?"

Ha!

And thus began our daily third period ritual, passing notes back and forth and supplying each other with gum and gossip. In time, I made it into the circle of cool kids—or the kids who thought they were cool—and dated some of the prince's best friends. Our notes evolved from frivolous banter to serious advice about our love lives.

And you still have those notes to show to your children!

By the middle of the school year, the prince and I were doing less than our best work in calculus class. So Mrs. Ragsdale had us transferred to separate *average* math classes. I was so offended when she told me that I needed to get my priorities straight. What could be more important than developing a relationship with this boy? Dear Mrs. Ragsdale, how silly you were!

You were the silly one...and your dad and I were not happy about your demotion in math!

On Friday and Saturday nights, you knew you were in the right place if the prince was there. Even when I was hanging on the arm of another boy, my stomach did a little flip when I'd see the prince, cigarette dangling from his alluring lips as he spun a tale for the crowd.

Oh, Mike!

There was one Saturday night in particular that I will never, ever forget. I was waiting for my ride to a party, and you and Dad had gone out to dinner. At fifteen years old, I was feeling quite mature so I decided to make myself a drink, a screwdriver. It was my first experience with liquor and I was surprised by how smoothly the vodka went down... I couldn't even taste it! Naturally, I made myself another and when my ride was late, I was feeling so good that I thought I'd make just one more for the road. I filled the vodka bottle up with water and headed out the door...

I knew it! Sneaky kid!

When we got to the party, I was drunk.

Big surprise.

And so disoriented that I ended up wandering aimlessly through the woods behind the house. It was the prince who came to my rescue, helping me into the house and up the stairs to sleep off my unfortunate error in judgement. He tucked me into a bed, looked down at me with those penetrating eyes, and left the room before I lost my lunch (and breakfast and dinner) all over the place. Not one of my finest hours...

No, but it was certainly one of his.

This heroic image was not what the prince usually projected. He was a bad boy in many respects—fist fights, car wrecks, even running from the police on one occasion. He was known for breaking laws and breaking hearts. Often the lead story in Monday's gossip chain, his name echoed through the halls… "He really pounded him this time," or "His second car totaled this year!" or "Poor Kathy… She walked in on him kissing another girl… She's devastated!"

Not my son-in-law!

When the prince was a senior and I was a junior, we went to prom together, me with his best friend, and he with his steady girlfriend, Katie. I still have the picture of the four of us, the prince and I sandwiched between our respective dates. He played the role of my hero again that night when my date ended up in a lip lock with another girl on the dance floor. Oh, the humiliation!

Oh, the drama!

Almost immediately, the prince swooped in and escorted me out to the parking lot, where we shared a good laugh. I don't remember what was funny, only that he illuminated a defining moment for me. I could break down…or cheer up. Our laughter lifted me. He lifted me.

He brought you home that night. A prince, indeed.

High school was over in a heartbeat. The prince and I went to different colleges, but after a year of pitiful grades (for him) and desperate homesickness (for me), the Universe brought us both to Virginia Commonwealth University, back to our hometown…

Back to the possibility of each other.

When I saw the prince at my nineteenth birthday party, my stomach did the same flip it did when I was fifteen. Over a six-pack of cheap beer, we flirted a bit and reminisced a lot, until the party's end, when he leaned in, channeled his sultriest soap opera voice, and asked me the question I'd been waiting to hear for a four-year lifetime, "May I kiss you?" I giggled. And we shared our first moment of sweet romance.

He promised to call me the next day. He promised to come over in the morning and help me clean up. Empty promises made by the prince who fell from his throne not twelve hours later. He never called and I ended up in the hospital when, in my frenzied attempt to destroy the party evidence before you and Dad got home, I cut my leg on a broken beer bottle. Probably his!

I came home from a relaxing weekend to find both a house and a daughter wrecked!

Sorry, Mom. You saw that my heart was broken and kindly withheld the speech I deserved.

You were a lucky young lady.

A year had passed when I ran into the ex-prince at another party, and as much as I tried to avoid him, his magnetic charm overpowered my good sense. I was cool toward him at first, reminding him of the phone call he never made. He offered a ridiculous excuse—something about fixing a vacuum cleaner for his parents—but he seemed genuinely sorry when I showed him the scar on my leg.

I bet he did. Hmmm…

And then he leaned in again, this time his moustache brushing my cheek and his warm breath a whisper in my ear, "You want to go out sometime?"

"Maybe," I said curtly, "but I won't be waiting by the phone this time."

Oh, that was good, honey.

The next day, the prince earned back his title when he called to set up our first date. He came to pick me up in his blue monstrosity of a car, affectionately nicknamed "The Blue Bomber." On a whim, we headed to the beach, hit a few bars, and then found ourselves wrestling in the sand, under a brilliant crescent moon. The prince stripped down to his tighty-whities to tackle the midnight waves. And, well, there was no other option but to join him. It's not safe to swim alone in the ocean!

Too much information, Nicki Beans.

We'd only been together a few months when I knew for sure that the prince was my forever one. It was Christmastime and I convinced him to play Santa Claus at the adult home where I was working. He was pure magic with my differently-abled friends. With a twinkle in his eye, just like the real Santa Claus, he sweat through his red suit and white beard, inviting each resident, even the ones who were twice his size, to sit on his lap and share their Christmas wishes. That's the night I knew I could spend the rest of my life with this man.

I knew too.

We began living in sin soon after that. It just made sense economically.

Sure, Nicki Beans.

Upon college graduation, we decided to take a cross-country trip together. Living in a car and a tent with someone for a month is certainly a test for a relationship, a test that we passed...even when I drove us three hundred miles out of our way, while he slept in the passenger seat, to visit the Laura Ingalls Wilder museum in historic Walnut Grove, Minnesota. I couldn't resist! But imagine the prince's surprise when he woke up expecting to be in Milwaukee for a night of bar hopping and instead found himself on the banks of Plum Creek in 1874.

Surprised, but tolerant of your strange ways. He couldn't deny your heart's desire. He still can't.

Two years into our courtship, I found the prince in the parking lot of the nursing home where I worked. He was all dressed up in a suit and tie, staring at me as if I were all that mattered in the world. He said that he had a romantic weekend planned for us, but that he just couldn't wait any longer. So it was in a nursing home parking lot, on a frigid December evening, with my senior citizen friends peering out the dining room window, that he got down on one knee, looked up at me with misty blue eyes, and asked me to be his wife. As he placed a ring on my finger, my eyes answered his. No words were necessary.

The language of soul Love, across lifetimes.

On January 6, 1996, the first day of the infamous Blizzard of '96, *the* prince became *my* prince, in an old church in Hampton, Virginia. After we vowed our vows and kissed our kiss, we walked outside into a winter wonderland where we danced in the silence of the snow, enchanted by the fairytale that was being written for us. At the reception, our best man, Patrick, made a toast that will be etched on my heart forever. He lifted his glass and recounted the events of the party three years earlier, where the prince had officially asked me out on our first date. Patrick told the crowd that the words the prince spoke that night were these: "I always knew, from the first day I saw her in math class, that someday Nicki would be my wife." All those years, all that gum…and all those other girls—they were just practice for me, the true love of his life, his princess…

What a beautiful story, Nicki Beans!

It's a true story, Mom…but it's not the whole story.

•••

Fairy tales always have a dark side, honey. And this one is no different. Mike was with you during the hardest time of your life, before medication, before we understood your struggle.

He witnessed my neurotic behavior and loved me anyway.

He saw through your conditioned psychology to your spirit, to the Truth of you.

On our cross country trip, he almost put me on a plane back home. There were days I couldn't stop crying. Days I needed constant reassurance that the little girl we saw at the coffee shop was not the missing child on the milk carton, that the bump we hit on the road was not a baby whose screams I could still hear, that my recurring nightmare was not a sign from God that I was a perverse monster who needed to be punished. My rational mind had abandoned me. I was drowning in a pool of karmic tears, my own and the world's, terrorizing myself…and the man I loved the most.

When you got home from your trip, Mike came with us to see the doctor. He held your hand as we listened to the explanation of obsessive compulsive disorder. He asked questions and took notes on ways he could help you cope with the condition… and ways he could cope.

He got a vivid picture of my potentially long-term challenges…and six months later, he still asked me to be his wife.

I loved the way he loved you…and continues to love you. He sees you, honey. All of you.

•••

I'm not sure your father ever fully saw me.

He saw the first beautiful layer of you, Mom. The one you allowed him to see in the beginning. But like an onion, you continued to reveal new layers of yourself. What was beneath your exquisite surface—your divine feminine power and innate wisdom—might have confused Dad, maybe even scared him.

I was a pretty package. Your dad liked pretty packages. As a young woman, I thought that's all I was. A turning point in my life was my first meeting with your grandmother, his mother. The judgement in her eyes was penetrating.

Well, she found you in her son's apartment, parading around in a bikini.

Probably not the best first impression on a woman as academic and cultured as your grandmother. She went to college at age sixteen and earned two master's degrees by the time she was twenty years old!

That must have been heavy information to hold, Mom, given your own insecurities around education.

Perhaps that's why I felt so angry under her condescending glare.

Anger is a gift, a disruptive reminder of what matters to us. Your intelligence mattered to you, Mom.

The theory of multiple intelligences had not yet been developed. Back then, being smart meant having a high IQ. Intelligence was defined as a general ability, which you either had or didn't have. And I didn't have it. So, I prided myself on how I looked and how I interacted with others, which I would learn later is called interpersonal intelligence. Spirit certainly gave me a large dose of that!

Undeniably!

What I perceived as your grandmother's judgement of my appearance and cheerful personality lit a fire in me and reminded me, on a soul level, that there was more to me than met the eye, more to discover…over time.

Once that fire was lit, you became more aware of Dad's worldview of intelligence and how he valued it in others.

I was hurt when he talked about different women at the office who were "so sharp." I know your father loved me for many reasons…but my intellect was not one of them. In our early years together, I don't know that he appreciated my own unique intelligence, in part, because I didn't fully appreciate it myself. But as I began to explore and honor my many layers, so did he…

We're all just doing the best we can.

That might be the most profound lesson we can learn in human form, honey. Resisting this Truth creates a lot of unnecessary suffering. People can only see and hear and feel what they are ready to see and hear and feel.

We're all on our own path to self and source realization.

While we can share the wisdom we gain on our path, we can't expect those we love to simply accept and embody it. We all learn in our own time, through our own experiences. Being present in the intersection of our paths, in whatever dynamic is unfolding, is the greatest gift we can offer to the people we meet on the journey.

Dad recognized the rapid rate of your evolution, Mom. He shared with me recently that the pretty little girl he married grew quickly into a confident and independent woman. He admitted that this was hard for him in some ways and liberating in others. Perhaps it was a challenge for him to see and hear and feel all of you, Mom. But he loved you as deeply as he could. Of this I am sure.

I am too, honey. We were a good team. Your dad was an excellent provider and I took care of everything and everybody at home. I was also a huge asset to your dad's career. He climbed the corporate ladder with me on his arm, shining at each and every Xerox function. We played the game, and it was fun. We had a real knack for balancing our career life, our family life…and our romantic life.

For me, there was a great deal of security in the schedules you both adopted, as well as the roles you both assumed. Our refrigerator was stocked and our home was neat and clean, thanks to you. Our yard was manicured and our cars were maintained, thanks to Dad. On Saturday mornings, Dad worked in the garage until I got up for our weekly trip to Hardee's for sausage biscuits. On Wednesday nights, you gave me a bubble bath and then presented me to Dad for a tickle fight and an episode of his favorite sitcom. Saturday nights were your date nights. With a gin and tonic in his hand and a sappy grin on his face, Dad watched you cascade down the stairs, Holly and me and a trail of perfume behind you.

He saw me...

...and he valued you, Mom. You both made sure Holly and I knew that the paycheck Dad brought home was as much yours as it was his.

I was his partner in every way. We needed each other. It was unsettling to listen to friends talk about the allowances they received from their husbands. As if they were children! The nerve of those men! They would have been nothing without their wives.

With a feminist spirit in a conventional world, you embodied the content, stay-at-home mom and the fiery, liberated woman. You could hold both. And you showed me that I could too.

•••

Around the time we moved to Virginia, I gained access to a trust fund established by Grandpa Parchman. I was thirty-five years old, and it was as if the world just opened up for me. As a result of your dad's promotion and my grandfather's gift, our socioeconomic reality was greatly enhanced. Our new neighborhood had a country club, for goodness sake, a much different scene than the cinderblock-lined recreation center we frequented in Ohio. We had a big yard and a screened porch. I was living the dream...of the dream.

Was there a part of you that felt intimidated by your new reality, Mom?

No, I was ready for more sophistication in my life. I traded in my bowling ball for a tennis racket. I enjoyed the country club lifestyle, and I was quite good at it for many years. I appreciated that you and Holly were being exposed to some finer things as well.

You were proud of what you and Dad had built.

I was, but I never forgot my roots. I never took for granted the money Grandpa Parchman left me. A hard working, overall-wearing farmer,

Grandpa was as proud of his radishes as he was of his real estate investments.

I wonder why he deemed thirty-five as the age you could access your trust.

Grandpa was a smart man. He knew that a bit of financial struggle in the early years of family life was essential to building a strong marital foundation. And he knew that for most, the mid to late thirties were a time of greater maturity and intention to invest in things that would last, as opposed to one's earlier years when the habit of spending impulsively would lead to certain loss.

What did that money mean for you, Mom?

It meant independence. While my marriage was solid and your dad rarely questioned my spending habits, a woman needs to know that she can take care of herself if necessary. My mom taught me that...

...and you taught Holly and me.

The money also contributed to my sense of self-worth. Like most of the human race, I carried the "I'm not enough" baggage, mine containing those old imprints of shame around my learning challenges. Imprints that continued to deepen through my interactions with your grandmother...and your dad, in some ways. I had so much to say, but often couldn't find my words. I longed for more respect than I received sometimes.

Along with Dad, Holly and I were big personalities, demanding your attention, your praise, your reassurance. We didn't allow you the time you needed to process and share your own thoughts. Yet you held us all with such patience, sacrificing your own voice by so deeply listening to ours.

My patience only went so far, honey. In my struggle to find my voice, my temper often flared.

Oh, that temper!

Some of it was genetic, my daddy coming through my form. And some of it was a symptom of my need to be seen and heard...and felt.

You deserved every bit of our respect, Mom. And we deserved every arm twist we ever received. With your teeth clenched and your eyes squinted, you would bring us to our knees with your grip.

It was good for you, honey. I have no regrets...

•••

Creating beauty was your life's work, Mom. Our home was an illustration of your gift.

Our home was my joy...and my job. Room by room, I made it beautiful. For me, the house was not only a reflection of my creative capabilities, but of my value as a wife and mother.

Every Christmas, Dad presented you with a "Best Homemaker Award," an acknowledgement of your beautiful work, work that often went unrecognized in our daily routines.

Your father loved his awards. He dedicated a whole wall to his plaques from Xerox and various civic organizations. He wanted me to have some framed accolades too.

He saw you, Mom...

...and he celebrated me.

Do you remember the red carpet on the stairs?

That carpet drove me crazy!

No matter how often you vacuumed, there was a sticky lint that always collected there. I have vivid memories of you climbing the stairs on your hands and knees, cursing under your breath, as you meticulously picked the carpet clean of any imperfection.

Perfectionism is part of our genetic programming, honey, the compulsion to maintain an appearance of perfect or at least very "nice," regardless of the reality of the situation.

And Dad's need for order was intense. If there was a pair of shoes out of place in the house, it would unsettle him. He'd sigh in exasperation...and you would put the shoes away.

I didn't want anyone to be unsettled. I believed it was my responsibility as a homemaker to keep things calm and as close to perfect as possible. I dismantled that belief eventually, but when you girls were young, that was my purpose. And purpose was essential to my sense of wholeness.

A picture of grace, you seemed to move through the cadence of your days with ease. From the time you woke up in the morning and enjoyed your first cup of instant international coffee…

I was very worldly.

There was rarely a rush in the morning. We seemed to fold into the day organically. You'd pack my lunch as you stole glances at *Good Morning America* on our little black and white TV on the kitchen counter.

I really liked the morning anchorwoman. She had a good sense of fashion.

You'd engage me in simple conversation as I picked apart my egg and sucked down my glass of powdered *juice*, if you could call it that.

You never ate the white part of your fried eggs. Why didn't I just scramble them? And you were addicted to that fluorescent orange sugar water. What was I thinking, buying that stuff?

I only liked the yellow part of the fried eggs, and the orange drink was my version of your international coffee.

You thought I wasn't looking when you put an extra scoop of powder in your glass. It's amazing your teeth didn't fall out of your head.

You'd hand me my lunch and my backpack and send me on my way to the bus stop. All hopped up on sugar, I'd skip down the driveway and look back at least three times to find you smiling and waving at the door.

Then I'd clean up the kitchen and make my plan for the day. There were always errands to run and calls to make and home projects to tackle. Sometimes there was a tennis match or a luncheon with my friends. I was never bored. I always had purpose.

And you made relaxation an imperative part of your day too. I often came home from school to find you outside in a lounge chair, with your eyes closed, soaking up the sun.

That was my meditation, long before I knew what meditation was. As soon as I'd hear your little feet on the gravel driveway, I'd get back back to my job…making you a snack, preparing what was necessary for dinner, helping with homework, taking care of whatever needed my attention in the house…

…like the lint on the red stairs!

That was my work, Nicki Beans.

•••

My life path number, the number established by adding the month, day, and year of one's birthdate, was six. No surprise that life path six, my numerological blueprint for this lifetime, indicates a focus on family and responsibility…and on nurturing one's own creativity. As you girls got older, I needed to tend my own summertime fire, apart from our family life in our lovely neighborhood, apart from the lint on the stairs. I was ready to go back to work, ready for some tangible recognition of my value, outside of my yearly "Best Homemaker Award."

With your interest in fashion and your fashion model appearance, retail was the ideal path for you to re-enter the working world after almost two decades at home. You gained some confidence working at a little shop in a strip mall before landing your dream job at fancy boutique.

The eighties were a flashy time to be in the fashion industry. Big shoulder pads, big belts, big earrings, big hair…and big credit card bills! I couldn't believe how weekly shopping sprees were the norm for some women. They would throw stacks of credit cards on the counter, not at all embarrassed by those that declined.

This was new territory for you, Mom. You were not of this reckless spending era. You stayed true to your family values throughout your life. You bought what you could afford. Period.

True…but I did buy a lot. Clothes were a way to express myself without words. And I had a lot to say.

You were the queen of the fashion statement.

Every time I purchased a new frock for myself, I would hear Grandpa Parchman whispering through the ether, words he often spoke when in form...

"That's it, Nance. Buy something pretty for yourself."

It wasn't that he was encouraging careless spending—the clothes I bought were designed to last. It was that he was honoring my freedom in the world. He was loving me, and giving me permission to express and love myself.

An enlightened man. Good ol' Hiney!

•••

Last night, I was curled up with some of your books on spirituality, looking for you in the pages.

Even when I was too tired to read, I would open a book to a random page and fold it over my heart, inviting the wisdom to fill me.

I found you in a passage about doing one thing at a time, and doing it absolutely.

That's how I lived most of my life, more an illustration of common sense than any deep wisdom. After all, we only have two hands, one heart, and twenty-four hours in a day. What else can we do but one thing at a time?

You tried to instill this common sense in me, reminding me throughout the summer of my life,

You can't have it all at once...

But I so wanted it all at once. I wanted the cute husband who adored me. I wanted the quaint house in the perfect neighborhood. I wanted three children in five years. I wanted to continue my teaching career. I wanted to be an activist in my community. I wanted to write inspiring articles. I wanted to shine on the storytelling stage. I wanted to lead circles and ceremonies. I wanted to look forever twenty-nine, but contain the wisdom of an eighty-year-old crone. I wanted to do unique and creative things in and for the world, while winning "Best Homemaker Awards" from my family.

So much wanting.

What I didn't want was to do just one thing at a time.

You exhausted yourself, honey. I knew, given your overactive and obsessive mind, that stillness was a liability for you and that staying busy had its benefits. But you had such high standards for yourself, always choosing the effort of doing over the peace of being.

It's ironic, really. Throughout the spring and into the summer of my life as a young mother, I was desperately attached to my flower child identity. Peace signs, tie-dyes, and sun salutations on the sideline of the soccer field were my jam. I thrived on my image as a tree-hugging, free spirit. Yet inside, I was far from peaceful. Far from free.

To cultivate true peace, one must be ready to explore their inner landscape. For you, going within carried the risk of bumping up against sticky and frightening thoughts... deluded stories that would lead you away from Truth, rather than toward it.

So I rested in the false safety of my identity and my to-do list. I became fluent in the language of Love and used it to help me achieve all my mind-generated goals. The artificial light of my spiritualized ego was in full force. But underneath, I could feel my natural, peaceful essence longing to be set free.

You were living in your head, honey. But your heart was waiting patiently for you. In time, you would find your way and your peace there.

In the mid-summer of my life, my core belief was still in control... "If I am good, I will be loved. If I am loved, I will be safe."

It is your life's work to dismantle this lie... to remember that you are loved— not for what you DO, but for who you BE.

•••

For my fortieth birthday, my dear friend Amanda organized a poignant tribute for me. I was standing in my kitchen early in the morning and, as if it were coming from Heaven, I heard my favorite song...

"This Little Light of Mine."

I glanced out my window to see a parade of angels—men, women, children, dogs—strolling down my street. Amy and Suzy of the coolest girl band in town, led the tribe of Light-filled singers to my doorstep. There I sat in a puddle of tears, accepting flowers from beautiful children and drinking in the Divine faces of the crowd.

A moment you will never forget.

And a moment of inner conflict. I am so lucky to be this loved, I thought...and I am not worthy of this Love.

You hadn't learned to love yourself.

A month after my birthday, I stopped taking my antidepressants and fell into a severe state of depression and anxiety.

Depriving yourself of your medication was an act of violence against your humanity.

I thought I had all the tools I needed to navigate my mental health. I thought the medicine was weakening my connection to Spirit, masking the Truth I needed to see.

But it was only strengthening your container of self, offering you the clarity necessary to function in the world.

In my effort to find the Truth I so desperately craved, I spiritually bypassed my body and its undeniable needs.

And that little Light of yours went out.

You drove down to see me, but all you saw was my pain. I collapsed in your embrace.

I took you to the pharmacy to get your medication. There were no words to speak.

You watched me take my little yellow pill. You held my hand and broke the silence with a whisper...

"There, now. It's going to be alright."

I stayed in bed for a long time. I couldn't eat. I couldn't sleep. Emptying the dishwasher was an accomplishment. Holly drove car pool while I sat in the passenger seat, my kids studying me with curiosity and concern.

They were well aware of your deep sensitivity and your raw vulnerability. You never hid your truth from them. But they couldn't reconcile this delicate woman before them with the capable woman they had always known, the woman who carried them in one arm while conquering the world with the other.

Mike held us all up during that time. He maintained his rigorous career in money management, while grocery shopping on his lunch breaks and attending school and sporting events in the evenings. He tucked the children in at night with promises that tomorrow would be better. Tomorrow I would be stronger.

He never once doubted that you would overcome this challenge, that your little Light would shine even brighter on the other side of it.

I had to quit my job at a leadership development collective where I taught children to love and honor themselves. I suppose my ears were deaf to my own voice.

We can only hear what we're ready to hear, Nicki Beans. This was part of your path. And this crisis came with a gift, as all disruptions do.

•••

It was during this tender time that I got my first glimpse of ultimate reality. I discovered the stillness underneath the noise and the space behind the thoughts. When I looked to the sky, I was no longer overwhelmed by its vastness. Rather, I found comfort in its unbounded mystery. I began to recognize that panic and anxiety carry the same sensation as expansion. And I wondered if this heightened vibration was simply a more attuned connection to Spirit. Just another reflection of Love. I took the time to sit in the reverence of this wisdom, while also honoring that my physical form needed some medicinal support to operate in the world.

You discovered the Heaven of your heart, honey...the beauty of your human imperfection within your Divine perfection.

As I moved through Life without structure or plans, I finally understood what my friend Kelly told me years before...

"Allow your doing to arise from your being."

So I got lost in the woods with my dog. I watched movies in the middle of the day. I wrote stories for the joy of it. I built a friendship with a homeless woman...

Angel.

I met her on your birthday, Mom. Which just happened to be her birthday too.

Serendipity...

I found Angel sitting on the rail of a busy street, surrounded by bundles of plastic bags that serve to insulate her from the noise of the world. The stray cats that live in the adjacent parking lot are her primary concern, and she's made it her job to keep them safe from the monster-sized rats that live there too. Despite her harsh conditions, Angel's eyes twinkle and her skin glows. She keeps her mass of silver hair tucked neatly in the hood of her faded blue sweatshirt. She is beautiful.

An angel.

Yes, and a cherished friend. At the height of my depression, I felt safe sitting with her, basking in the warmth of the sun and watching the cars go by. Without roles or responsibilities, we were just two humans sharing time and space.

Sharing peace.

We've had some adventures in the world together too. Shopping and lunching and even visiting an RV lot to explore the possibility of a home for her. Over time, Angel has become part of my family, woven into the fabric of our lives. She thanks me a lot. But it is she who deserves my gratitude.

Through loving her, you learned to love yourself.

Being with Angel helped me understand and embody the African philosophy of Ubuntu...the unique expression of self within the web of Oneness.

I am because we are.

Once my medication started working again, I threw myself into creating compassionate communities through Ubuntu storytelling circles, Earth Love efforts, and a Grow Gratitude movement. The manifester in me re-emerged rather quickly, ready to create, ready to get back to the business of life.

You've got some of that fiery Leo in your astrological chart, honey. Stillness was not a long-term option. But your actions were becoming more aligned with your growing awareness.

When I returned to teaching and the drama of a school setting, I tried to stay awake to my awareness. But it was all too easy to reattach to the illusory importance of achievement, both for myself and for my students. I did carry some wisdom into my new second grade classroom and helped to create a mindful community that celebrated the wholeness of each child and the wholeness of our learning circle. But it was more effort than allowance, more of my spiritualized ego at work. The imprint of infinite possibility, however, made its mark on me. I had taken my first steps on the path toward abiding awakening. We can't unsee what we've seen.

Life is a journey of first steps, Nicki Beans. Beginning again and again, moment after precious moment...

•••

I worried about my children during my depression. Would this departure from stability overshadow the happy springtime of their lives?

By being open with them about your challenges, you gave them space to discover and deepen their own capacity for compassion and resilience.

I like to think it made them stronger. And perhaps more grateful for what we have as a family. When Grace was fourteen years old, she wrote a poem about her childhood. I cry every time I read it...

Beginnings

I come from tradition,
mountains high
miles wide.
Stronger than bitter December winds,
more precious than the roof over our heads.

I come from "because I said so"
and pixie dust.
From fairy houses
to tree houses
eleven years, standing strong,
because no dream is unreachable.

I come from long summers
and even longer bike rides.
From strawberry popsicles
To powdered lemonade stands,
Plastic pitcher and all.

I come from pruney fingers and green hair.
From mermaids and front flips,
blue lips,
community.

I come from hamburger buns and soggy charcoal.
From a dark rainstorm
that only lightens the mood.
From tents and cold hot tubs,
muddy feet and curly hair,
under a waterfall
ten below.

I come from median fireworks
and a few empty kegs.
Live music
and early mornings
with a barbeque smoker and a pig.
I am from bike parades and hula-hoop contests,
red white and blue frosting.

I come from a CVS umbrella and hurricane season.
From hot rain and biting sand
and a bowling alley.
I'm from a place where sunshine is a privilege
and the days are numbered,
but it's never less than magic.

I come from yellow cake with chocolate icing.
From princess gowns
to bell bottoms,
a candle per year.
I am from the final goodbyes of summer-
warm fall days,
auburn leaves.

I come from FedEx field tailgates
and buffalo chicken dip.
From a team loved because of our roots,
not their trophies.
I'm from Sunday afternoons,
burgundy and gold
and yet another loss.

I come from a saw and a hayride.
From pumpkins
to Christmas trees,
straight from the ground.
I come from boiling apple cider
and bonfires
to mask the brisk mountain air.

I come from a rainy Friday,
and Ukrops fried chicken.
A baby cradle,
two months too soon.

I come from a little yellow house
With a black lab
a big oak
and a baby swing,
swung into sweet beginnings.

•••

My Grace. She was two months too soon.

And when I called to tell you that I was going in for an emergency cesarean section, you said,

No, she's not due until November. It's only September. And I just took a Tylenol PM.

You missed the birth of the first, Mom, but you were there for the next two.

Holly was there too. Mike said we should set up bleachers.

He fussed a bit about having you both in the delivery room, but deep down, he loved the closeness we all shared. He wouldn't have had it any other way.

Witnessing the birth of your children was among the greatest honors of my life. The miracle of birth cannot be described in words. The miracle of your own child giving birth is beyond what the human heart can hold.

•••

Having three children under five years old must have been challenging, honey.

It was a comedy of errors, Mom. Recently, I walked by our budding azalea bush and stopped to reminisce. In my mind's eye (or perhaps my heart's eye), I could see them there, ages one, three, and six, posing for a picture in their Easter best. I stared at the pink blossoms and welcomed the deluge of memories that washed over me—not the sentimental ones as reflected upon in Grace's poem…but the ones I'd rather not claim, the ones that make me laugh out loud. I remembered…the questionable placement of the bourbon next to the breast pump on the kitchen counter; Grace uttering her first clear word, "Beer!"; Mike putting Viv's high chair, with Viv in it, on the porch when she wouldn't stop screaming at dinner; Rhode's habitual nudity until well into his fourth year; our family mantra when things went wrong, as coined by Viv for her sister, "Stupid Dumb GaGa"; and finally, the kids and I sitting outside the bedroom door, a week after Mike's vasectomy, waiting for him to *finish* so we could take the sample to the doctor.

So much laughter… I loved watching you raise your family, honey.

In Truth, they are raising me, Mom.

You are raising each other, creating a garden of memories that grows wilder with every passing year. There will always be some weeding to do, but the beauty of your garden is in the unique and random way you each grow...and grow together.

Ubuntu.

I've made and will continue to make lots of mistakes. Sometimes I think I've projected too much of myself onto my children. Other times, I worry I haven't shared or exposed them to enough.

Children are born with Divine intelligence, the seeds of Love embedded in their hearts. It is not our job to teach them...

...but to remind them of what they already know.

•••

Home Church was a sweet experiment for your family...

...an idea sent by Spirit. Instead of getting dressed for church on Sunday mornings, we stayed in our pajamas for Home Church. Sitting around a candle, taking turns with the singing bowl to initiate our "service," we shared our challenges and triumphs of the week and our intentions around how we would be better humans in the week to come. Sometimes there would be questions to explore or a clip of a movie to discuss, but mostly it was just a time to be together, to see ourselves and each other in a deeper way. The best Home Church services were the ones led by the kids, at random.

You could be a little serious, honey, a little too structured. Their ideas brought levity...and some fun!

The girls would blast their favorite boy band on the house speakers and we'd all dance and sing like rock stars before collapsing in our circle for a child-inspired activity. Like drawing flowers, which Grace explained reflected qualities in each of us that were asking for our attention. Or collective finger painting that Viv recognized as an illustration of Ubuntu. Or making up rap songs because Rhode liked to make up rap songs.

You extended Home Church to include us—your dad and me and Holly and Dave.

The Together Tour! I loved coming up with catchy names. My busy mind at work again.

The mind is not a bad thing, honey. You depend on it more than is necessary, but it has served you well...and served your family well. I cherished the Together Tour! We took turns planning experiences, some of which were playful like bowling and touch football. And some more sacred, like foot-washing, feeding one another, caring for the graveyard at Idylwood, and burying a time capsule of memories—this memory being the most enduring of all.

Nature created the most vibrant patches on our metaphorical family quilt. There were full moon fire circles, solstice celebrations, and early morning hikes to the river. We hugged trees and built fairy houses and sought guidance from the nature spirit oracle cards and healing stones on our coffee table, our family altar.

Through these simple, natural, and real experiences, you've helped your children remember that God not only lives inside of them, but in everyone and everything of the Earth.

Maybe. I hope so. Viv has made some new friends in high school who are very involved with their church youth groups. Recently, she questioned her lack of religious training and commented that she doesn't know anything God.

I know that broke your heart.

I got a little defensive, reminding her that we are nothing but God; that we are spiritual beings having human experiences; that we honor God by taking the time to reflect on our humanity, together as a family; that to be in authentic relationship with each other is the clearest reflection of our relationship with Spirit; that the experience of being in a family, as an essential part of all its messy dysfunction, is really our most powerful spiritual practice; that when we show up to this experience with Love and openness, then and only then do we truly know God...as us.

And you lost her ten seconds into your rant.

Yep. Too much, huh? Why do I do that?

Less is almost always more, honey. Especially with teenagers.

When Grace was Viv's age, we took a faith exploration class at church together. It was a deepening experience, but in the end, Grace determined that she didn't want to be confirmed in the Episcopal Church. She wasn't ready to make that commitment. I was proud of her self-awareness— proof that she had, indeed, come in already taught by Spirit. Maybe Viv needs the same opportunity to explore her faith.

Maybe. And you can trust that she's got everything she needs already within her. Church is not the only answer. It provides stories that point to some Truths. It is not Truth itself.

I hope, if they remember nothing else, they remember our bedtime prayer,

"God is Love. So am I. Love is all there is. Thank you."

This is all they need to know.

•••

Once upon no-time, you made a contract with your family of five to travel through lifetimes together, supporting each other on your individual soul journeys. As a soul family, you picked the roles and challenges that would play out in this lifetime.

What a privilege it is be in a family. To be in intimate relationships with other humans, whose karma, across lifetimes, is intricately entwined with my own. To look into the eyes of my husband and children and see the infinite beings they are, the infinite web of connections we share.

It's hard to stay in the Truth of this expansive space in the day to day of human dynamics.

Nearly impossible. I spend a fair amount of time in resistance to what is, striving to direct the flow of my loved ones' lives. I try to respect their soul agendas. I know I can take no credit for their beauty, just as I can accept no blame for their trials. These are their blessings to cultivate and their dragons to tame.

At best, you are a witness and an ally on their journeys.

But I want to be their protector, to keep them safe from harm.

Setting boundaries is your responsibility as a parent, but ultimately, you must remember that you are not in control.

A reminder I get every time we get lice...

Those little bugs have found their way to your family's heads many times... Spirit knows what you need.

Parenting is so gray. A black and white manual for each child would be nice.

Your children are the walking, talking manuals. They are your teachers.

Grace has a willful, risk-taking personality. I worry about the trouble she might attract in her life.

Not in your control. She is a child of the wild. Let her show you how to embrace joy with abandon. She is a force of Life, an old and wise soul.

Viv has a sensitive vibration. I worry that she will be overwhelmed by the chaos inherent in the world.

Not in your control. Let her show you how she rises above the noise. She is learning to tame her dragon and make it her friend. She is stronger than you know.

Rhode struggles deeply with the physical and emotional aspects of diabetes. I worry that he will miss out on the sweetness Life has to offer.

Not in your control. Give him time and he will chart his own course, creatively navigating this chronic condition that has many lessons for him. He will show you the way.

Everyday they wake up, they are different.

And everyday you get the chance to remember the promises you made with them...in no-time.

•••

You were the best Nonie to my children.

I was the memory maker.

Our time away together was such a gift, one that you funded every year. Key West holds many of our family chronicles.

Our home away from home. Serenity...

...the name of the house that sheltered us for twelve years and the state of extreme *being* for which this gem of an island allowed.

I can still see us walking through the gate, around the tree-lined path that opened to our little paradise. The lagoon-like pool, the exotic flowers, the elegant decor of the house itself...

It was a dream...

...inside of our dream.

Around that pool was where I iced my swollen breasts when Rhode decided he was finished with nursing.

It's where you picked lice out of each other's heads like monkeys.

It was an assembly line of Love.

It's where we had talent shows and played gin rummy...and where the guys and Holly drank gallons of beer.

It's where we explored our humanity and our Divinity and the challenge of holding both simultaneously.

Oh Nicki... It would have served you well to have indulged in a few more beers!

Vacation was hard for me. As much as my body and spirit needed the pause, my attachment to my thoughts and my drive to understand the meaning of Life was accelerated during any free time.

Seeking the meaning of Life is futile, honey. Because you are Life. In every emerging and fading moment. There is nothing to seek.

Such a slippery Truth.

Thank goodness for your kids. They kept you present on vacation.

Even though we were only there for one week of the year, it seems my children grew up on the infamous Duval Street, amidst the colorful locals, the drunken tourists, and the bold and beautiful drag queens—one of whom we befriended. The kids got an inside view of Jessie's life… and her dressing room!

You and Mike welcomed opportunities to expose your children to diversity.

In Key West, they learned to crawl and walk and swim and dance…

We made memories that left eternal imprints on our hearts.

Remember our matching Free Hugs shirts?

Nothing like spreading Love on Duval Street. And our EGGSperiment?

It was Easter and each of us put a love note inside a plastic egg, with a message at the end to "pass it on." Rhode gave his to a random couple at a restaurant. As they read their sweet message from my seven-year-old boy, the man began to cry. Above the noise, the woman said to me, "Your son is beautiful. Ours passed away two weeks ago." And for the next half hour, my son and this couple shared popcorn, jokes…

…and the joy of a not so random human connection.

Serendipity…

•••

Over the years, you cultivated profound and enduring relationships with your grandchildren. As little ones, they looked to you for your unconditional devotion, your pride in their beingness. And as they grew, they came to you for your wisdom…or it was given to them, whether they asked for it our not.

Like the speech about gratitude I delivered on the streets of Key West?

They needed to hear it. All of Key West needed to hear it!

My grandchildren, my angels, were acting like brats! They needed some valuable reminders of what it means to be in a family...considering the feelings of everyone, giving as much or more as receiving, and offering gratitude from the heart, always from the heart.

A dose of Nonie wisdom is precious.

A little bit of a temper, a little ranting every now and then, is good for children.

You are good for children.

Thank you, honey.

We tried going back to *Serenity* after you passed, Mom. I knew you were there...but without your sweet scent, your adorable laughter, the vision of you in your straw hat and big sunglasses, our dream inside the dream was tainted.

It was too soon. Your children, when they are no longer children, will bring you all back to Key West. There will be new memories made there and I will be in the texture of each one.

In our family vacation journal, we found your words and the timeless message they carried...

"Each family member makes the puzzle complete, each piece large and small, so needed to complete our circle of love."

You'll never stop creating circles, will you, Mom?

Nope. Never.

•••

The first line of Grace's poem is, "I come from tradition..."

...what Mike values more than anything. Tradition holds people together, he says.

There were and continue to be many annual events that are non-negotiable in our house.

Vacations, like our spring break in Key West, a tradition that will be born again…

And our beach week at Sandbridge with our best friends.

Where we went when you were a little girl…with our family friends.

All the way from Ohio in the station wagon!

How wonderful that you continued the Sandbridge tradition with your own family…minus the station wagon.

Another circle, Mom.

And there's your Fourth of July party.

Mike loves this celebration. For him, it begins in the wee hours of the morning when he rises to fire up the grill for the seventy-five pounds of pig products he's brined for the occasion. By late afternoon when the band arrives to set up in the treehouse, Mike is manic with anticipation. His frenetic energy carries him to night's end when he presents an illegal and unrivaled fireworks show in the front yard, that usually prompts a visit from the police.

He thrives on the mayhem…and the memories he creates each year.

He's a memory maker like you, Mom. While I usually resist this tradition and the prospect of over a hundred people in my backyard, I'm always happy on the fifth of July as I remember the barefoot frolicking with happy children waving enchanted sparklers; the inevitable thunderstorm that drives herds of sweaty and smiling people inside to leave soggy hot dog buns in my couch; the drinking and laughing and dancing with my sister and other kindred spirits in the brilliant dusk sunshine or in the pouring rain; and the rainbow that sometimes appears in the wake of the storm.

There's always a rainbow, honey. Sometimes, you just have to look harder for it.

And then there's Christmas…

…the most magical time of year.

Well, Santa Claus is our great-great-great-grandfather. Remember, Mom? I'm named for him—Saint *Nick*!

Ah yes, I remember. The story you told your children—and all their friends—that they never doubted, until the sad day that they did. The story of our visit to the North Pole, when Santa was sick with the flu. The story of how you saved Christmas by helping the elves with a debacle at the doll-making station. The story of your love for Santa Claus, who just happens to be your great-great-great-grandfather.

The story I told so many times that I started to believe it. Really, who's to say it's not true, in an alternate reality or in a parallel life?

It held a lot of magic for a lot of years, honey. Might be time to tuck it away for now…

Maybe so, Mom. Even without the story, the wonder of Christmas still lives at our house. On the first Saturday of December, Mike puts on his grandfather's railroad overalls and the five of us head out to a tree farm with our best friends, a cooler of Mike's homemade, mind-blowing eggnog, and a wide open day ahead of us. We spend hours roaming the fields, singing songs, taking family pictures that never make it on the Christmas card...and arguing over which tree will come home with us. When a consensus is met, I ask the chosen evergreen if it's willing to be ours while Mike shows our boy how to use the saw.

With the tree on top of the car, we head to a pizza joint that hopefully has a jukebox. We slide with ease into vinyl booths and comfortable banter with our best friends. After six throwback songs, three greasy pizza pies, and a couple pitchers of flat beer, we finally make our way home with the ambitious goal of decorating our new green friend that night.

Every year, Mike wrestles the tree off the car and looks at it skeptically, "Hmm, it didn't look this big on the lot… I'll have to do some trimming." An hour later, after a few battles with lights that don't work (but did when we put them away the previous year), Mike says he's calling it a day.

The five of us sprawl out in the family room and watch *It's a Wonderful Life*, with our chocolate lab named George Bailey curled up at Mike's feet. We only make it about halfway through the movie before we're all sound asleep.

That's a lovely vision of your family.

For me, it's an eggnog-induced sleep. Christmas Tree Day is the one day of the year I allow myself to let go and get totally schnockered.

Good for you, honey.

The Christmas traditions continue with our annual caroling party. Primed with Mike's eggnog, we parade with our friends to the neighborhood retirement home, where we serenade the gracious seniors who are kind enough to open their doors to us. Our hearts break and burst with each song as our listeners' eyes reflect the memories of Christmases past.

Your gratitude chain is my favorite holiday ritual.

A couple weeks before Christmas, the five of us sit around the fire with colored strips of paper, sharpies, and a stapler. We write what we are thankful for on the strips and then staple our blessings together to form a chain that drapes across the kitchen window...

Then you take it apart on Christmas night, rereading each blessing and offering it to the fire in prayer.

The room gets so hot that we have to strip down to our underwear!

Mike loves his big fires!

Since you passed, Mom, we keep the chain up until your birthday in September. Then we build a fire outside and release our blessings, faded from the sun and infused with nine months of family memories.

I will always be there for that tradition!

•••

One year, in the wake of my deep dip (as I've come to understand depression), we skipped our Sandbridge vacation to do something different.

Belize!

It was a stretch for Mike and the kids, given that we also skipped the Fourth of July bash that season to go camping as a family instead.

You needed some space. When a tradition is strong, it can afford a year off. When families are strong, they rise to support each other's needs.

I wanted us to do something meaningful together, something beyond our collective comfort zone. I found an orphanage in Belize where we could volunteer as a family.

And you invited me.

There was no question that this experience was for us to share, Mom. I envied the trips you and Holly took together, although I didn't have the desire to join you. I was happiest at home.

You traveled miles within yourself, just sitting on your couch with a baby in your lap.

My sense of adventure has been slower to awaken in this lifetime, but I came in with a strong sense of purpose. For me, our Belize trip was an ideal mix of big purpose and a little adventure.

For me too, honey. The children we met at the orphanage left their signatures on my soul, as did the caregivers with whom I worked. I saw such beauty and potential in these women. We saw it in each other.

After your kitchen shift, you and your coworkers would sit in a circle, unconcerned by any socioeconomic or cultural barriers, united by the spirit of the Divine feminine pulsing in each of you.

I'd look up to see you strolling by with a baby in a carriage.

Such peace on those strolls. Such contentment.

My grandchildren learned how to speak Creole and shake mangos out of trees.

They learned to appreciate the simple pleasures of sharing a soda, reading a book aloud, and sitting quietly in the sun with another child—so different from themselves, yet not different at all.

Nothing to do, but be…

…while Mike was castrating pigs and working the land with Mr. T, the caretaker of the place.

He treasured every second of it.

The kids rubbed his bald head and called him Big Daddy.

We played baseball, painted nails, made hula hoops, roasted marshmallows, and danced in the moonlight.

We cried when we left. Love had cracked us wide open…

…and the Light poured in.

Ubuntu. We are each brilliantly unique... and we are One.

•••

The winter of your life began shortly after our return from Belize. Your illness stole the sweetness of my summertime, Mom.

A bitter taste of the inevitable.

What was it like for you...in the winter of Grandma's life?

Grandma struggled with arthritis for many years, but her condition escalated after we moved to Virginia.

We saw Grandma and Grandpa nearly every season. Grandma moved a little slower from year to year, but I never remember her being sick. I loved when they visited us. On the day of their arrival, I would race home from the bus stop, eager to sing Grandma the song I'd been practicing for her. I'd lead her to the couch across from the hearth that was my stage, and she would smile her sparkling smile and implore me to sing my song over and over again.

Mom adored you and your sister. She couldn't be anything but happy in your presence. But her smile covered her pain, honey. I knew her mobility was becoming a greater challenge, but even I didn't know the extent of her suffering.

When did she finally tell you, Mom?

She didn't. I got a letter from her next door neighbor.

That must have been hard to read.

There was a web of anger, guilt, and despair that I tried to untangle for years, before and after her death. How could she or Daddy or my sister not have told me…and how could I not have asked?

You took several trips to Ohio to be with her.

It became obvious that the arthritis was slowly crippling her body, and the various medications she was taking to manage her pain were creating other complications.

Her heart.

Yes…her heart was weakening.

And her spirit?

Still vibrant.

Amazing.

Given Mom's pure spirit, I wonder if she had long since transformed the artificial light of our genetic design into her own holy rays of Truth. Perhaps, she had never denied her pain…she had simply chosen not to struggle against it.

She had chosen not to suffer.

At the height of her illness, she was able to tap into something greater than herself, something beyond her physical discomfort. In awe, I watched her expand so that she could hold all of it—the pain, the joy, the Love that surrounded her. While she found peace with her condition, I still couldn't accept it.

That sounds familiar.

We walked a similar path together, didn't we, honey?

But unlike you, Grandma didn't have the knowledge of different healing modalities or the desire to seek alternative options or opinions. Hers was the generation that followed the doctor's orders. Period.

Before I could accept her condition, I had to question her choices.

You had a lot of questions.

I created a lot of disruption. But it was too late. I thought that if I had known sooner, I could have helped her. I could have saved her.

And now you know the Truth.

We are all part of a Divine play.

We are not in control.

This is the lesson we learn over and over again throughout our lives. In the end, it finally becomes clear, and we allow ourselves to surrender and rest in the mystery...

...while others continue to question and argue with reality. Holly and Dad and I questioned your path, Mom—as well-researched, intentional, and sacred as it was. In the end, we had to wonder... What if you had made different choices? But your inspired awareness was bigger than our doubt, and it radiated through your smile, your gaze, your touch.

There aren't words big enough to explain the mystery of Life or to penetrate the despair of those who are being left behind. But the Light that shines from those who have embodied the Truth is a transmission for those open enough to receive it.

I think I got it, Mom.

You're still getting it, honey. This is a process. There's always another layer...

•••

For me, summer's luster also faded with my children's overnight transformation into teenagers.

Ah, yes...the dog days of summer.

During those months of spending long weekends with you, I would come home on Monday nights and fall into my husband's waiting arms. But there were no little feet racing to greet me at the door.

Those little feet got big, honey...and carried your babies out into the world.

Which is what we want as parents...strong, independent, happy kids.

But you needed their presence and their warmth more than anything during that time.

With the passage of each year, my understanding of what it means to be a parent deepens.

That never ends...

I spent the early days with each of my children in a hypnotic trance—part sleep deprivation, I'm sure, and part Divine transmission of bliss. Nothing mattered but the mystical bond I shared with this tiny human. There was no boundary between us... I was the baby and the baby was me. Meeting the needs of this reflection of Spirit, this son or daughter of Light, was all that mattered...

Such a beautiful and brief season. When our children are babies, it feels impossible that they would ever leave us. Or that they would ever want to leave us. For a moment, we are their everything.

It took longer than usual for the nub of Rhode's umbilical cord to fall off...as if he, too, were holding onto this season with me, for me. And on Viv's fifth birthday, she declared, "I wish we don't have more birthdays...so we don't grow up and leave each other."

You've kept those words tucked in your heart...

...as sweet memory. Now, each birthday is a celebration of their individuation and a reminder that they will indeed grow up...and leave. Throughout their young lives, I have applauded each child's evolving sense of self, but also grieved for the loss of the union we once shared.

We are the vessels through which our children pass... We are the spectators of their joy and their longing.

I had a dream of being both the child and the mother at once...only knowing myself as part of you, my mother, and only knowing my children as part of me.

A boundless tapestry of Love.

Resting in this pure awareness of Oneness, I could see the illusion of separation. It was so clear.

We are all One, honey...but we need to function as individuals in this world we've created. All of it Life is God's poetry. Even the parts that hurt.

For parents, the poetry of adolescence hurts a lot. It is dissonant, hard on the ears and heart.

This is the child's intention. As she steps more firmly into herself, she must push you a few steps away.

I'm taking my children's cues with greater allowance, Mom. And stepping back with greater ease. On a recent family vacation, I watched my daughters dancing together under a full moon. Normally I would have inserted myself into their joy, but this time, I just basked in the glow of it. I was simply their witness.

As you step away from your children, you gain the space to move more completely into yourself. In this way, the process of letting our children go is a gift.

I am more than my roles of child and mother.

Honey, you are infinite. As you stride into this next season, remember that you not only belong to yourself, but the self belongs to the vastness that is you.

•••

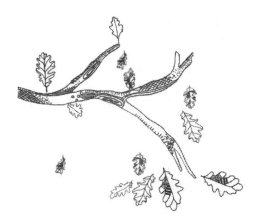

Autumn

•••

Can you hear the call of fall, Mom? Let's put on our fuzzy sweaters and whirl with the leaves in the wild wind. Let's dance our way back to our pristine origins and offer ourselves to Mother Earth.

A perfect day to invite the clean, crisp air to inspire us. How I miss breathing!

Now you are the breath. The formless. Pure Spirit.

The physical act of breathing is Spirit's greatest gift to humanity. It is a holy reminder of our Divinity, our eternal communion with God.

I will honor the breath, Mom…as I honor you.

•••

Just look at our Oakley, in all his glory.

He is a psychedelic celebration! Let's climb him, Mom, and sit on his branches. Let's lose ourselves in his cloak of color.

This is fun! I feel like a kid again. Little Curly Top is here to play!

I love climbing trees…being held by the arms of ancient awareness and seeing the world through a wider lens.

In the autumn of our lives, we gain perspective. We discover the depth of our color, the fullness of our Light.

We acknowledge each leaf on our tree as a vibrant story of our lives…

…and then we let our stories fall away.

By shedding the stories that have defined us, we create space for Spirit, space for our awakening.

Falling into nothing, we discover everything.

While the lines between each season are blurry, the passage into autumn is most elusive.

As we grow older and wiser, we recognize the illusion of lines. Life is a spiral. From birth to death, from lifetime to lifetime, we carry each season within us.

I am the innocent child, the passionate young woman, and the contemplative crone.

Hold them all with tenderness, honey. And breathe…

•••

When a mother dies, the child, no matter how old, must embrace her autumn. She must watch her most precious leaf, her most defining story, fall away…

It was a breezy November afternoon. The leaves on the trees were quivering in the sun's fading glow, ready to return to their source…when Aunt Joy called to tell us that Grandma was in the hospital.

I heard the news, but it was as if it was being relayed to someone else. Like I was watching some other pretty woman standing in her kitchen—a phone to her ear, a beagle at her feet, and a fourteen-year-old daughter by her side.

We left the next morning for Cincinnati. I don't remember the twelve-hour drive.

There was a lot of silence.

It was late when we got to the hospital. Grandma was too weak to offer her signature greeting. But I heard it through the ether, "Who's comin?" It's us, Grandma, I wanted to shout—to wake her up, to make her smile. Grandma didn't look like Grandma. And you, standing over her, didn't look like you.

I looked like her.

You were a reflection of her softness, her kindness.

She passed within the hour of our arrival.

She had waited for us.

For the three of us. Holly was in Germany for a year of study abroad.

Another step into autumn…when the first child flies far away.

Holly still regrets her absence for this profound moment. Yet the texture of death transcends the physical. She was there in every way that mattered.

As a young teenager, I couldn't feel the weight of death, or maybe I denied the feeling, distracting myself with my own immediate needs. I asked Dad if I could get some crackers from the vending machine. Or did I want pretzels?

Just like your children provided levity around my deathbed, you did the same around your grandmother's.

Another circle.

There's always another circle, honey…

•••

Five months after Grandma passed away, we took a trip to visit Holly in Germany.

And my daddy came with us. A return to his Deutsch roots.

What an adventure we had…beginning in the airport terminal when you—in your dark shades, your long, black trench coat, and your tall, black boots—got the major shake-down from airline security.

They thought I was some kind of a terrorist!

They thought you were sexy and took advantage of their position to put their hands on you!

Oh, Nicki Beans… Well, actually, you might be right.

We could see Holly waiting for us at the gate, her smile a beacon, her joy so buoyant she could have been carried away by the bouquet of balloons she held in her hand. When you were finally released by security, you dashed to your oldest daughter, your trench coat flying behind you.

I fell into her arms.

And she into yours.

It had been seven months since Holly left, but it felt like an eternity. Who was this grown woman-child before me? She had always been fiercely independent, but even I was surprised by the confidence she exuded in this foreign land. It was beyond her ability to speak the language. It was in her walk and her eagerness to move through unfamiliar territory, to be among diverse people. I knew then that she would be a perpetual wanderer and seeker of wonder. I was immensely proud of her, but also heavy with grief over the loss of my little girl…

…and the loss of your mom. It was too much. So you smiled through your tears…

…and delighted in every moment of this family adventure.

You let me sip on German beer.

When in Rome…or in Germany.

And I loved it!

Oh, I remember. Your sips quickly evolved into gulps! My fourteen-year-old was a happy drunk. You made your grandpa laugh. It was good.

Grandpa and I had an elementary command of the German language and we weren't afraid to use it...

...especially after a half pint of dark beer!

"Mehr bier, bitte (More beer, please)!" And Grandpa, when reading signs, didn't even attempt a German accent... "What the hell is 'Bad oder Dusche' (Bath or Shower)?"

Which was obscene in his Cincinnati vernacular. Oh, the gift of the giggles!

We went to the Baths in Baden-Baden, where we got naked in public and were salt scrubbed raw by aggressive women named Olga and Gerda.

You were hilarious.

I was traumatized!

As much fun as we had, my daddy's deteriorating health cast a shadow on our experience.

His heart broke when Grandma died.

And he had no desire to mend it.

You would lose another parent within the year.

While the trip may have strained Daddy's fragile heart, I have no regrets. It was the last call for our beer-loving patriarch.

With pride, he toasted Holly's embrace of our family roots on Earth...

...before returning to his beloved in Heaven.

• • •

My late springtime and your early autumn intersected in perfect time, Mom.

We found ourselves on many of the same paths in our pursuits to learn and grow. As I explored my multitudes, you and your sister were my greatest teachers.

And you were ours. Remember the Gerontology class we took together?

It was an experience that shifted my perspective on the classroom. Once a place of shame, with you it transformed into a place of possibility.

You rose to your power in that classroom, Mom. You sat in front of me, in the first row, and I smiled every time your hand shot up to share one of your wise insights. I was so proud of you.

We volunteered at an adult home together, leading activities for the folks at Ms. Buchanan's.

They especially enjoyed the boom box and we turned it up full blast, much to the chagrin of the head nurse, Ms. Tucker! A mixtape of soul-stirring songs blared through the speakers, sparking an hour of twisting and twirling through the dining room. Our dancing queens, Shelby and Margie, held nothing back, leading every conga line and inspiring even the most sedentary residents to clap their hands and sing along to the popular hip-hop tunes of the day. By the end of the hour, even Ms. Tucker was busting her moves!

Dancing with Shelby and Margie, in all their joy, woke me up to my joy...and to a new calling. I left my job at the fancy boutique for a position as an assistant activities director at a retirement home.

It was a perfect fit. Your Light shone through your service, Mom. You touched many hearts...

As I engaged with my new friends, I became more present, more aware of my capacity for compassion. Beyond my own fulfillment, this experience was also a bridge to my parents and grandparents, an opening to connection beyond death. My labor was an expression of my love for them.

You honored them with this holy work.

And I honored the deeper layers of myself.

•••

It was Dad's dream to live by the water.

Water is his element. Those dreamy, ocean-blue eyes of his were always searching for the sea. It brought him peace. And his peace was my peace.

It was no surprise that shortly after I left for college, you and Dad began planning your great escape to the Chesapeake Bay.

The empty nest of your childhood home was…empty. Your dad and I needed a new horizon. We needed a project that united us beyond raising our family. We would design and build a home on the water.

It took courage to leave everything you'd known for over a decade. To start anew.

It was another big step into the autumn of my life—perhaps more like a fall—into the unknown. It sounds dramatic, but the disruption of change, regardless of its appearance, is always challenging.

Shortly after your move to the water, you threw a birthday bash for Dad and me. His fiftieth and my twenty-first were just a day apart. On the boat, at the beach…we had a blast (and way too much beer)!

Well, my parties are pretty unforgettable, honey.

This is true, Mama. Yet what I remember most about the weekend was our good-bye. You, Holly, and I—sun-kissed, hungover, and holding back tears—leaned against Holly's VW bus, prolonging the inevitable. It didn't feel right, leaving you in this place. As beautiful as it was, it wasn't home.

There was confusion in this tender moment as we recognized the transition of us. We did not stand there as a mother and her daughters. Instead, we had become a trine of three women walking three different paths…yet, forever and always, walking each other home.

We realized that home was not a place.

Home was and still is…us.

And no matter where we each find ourselves, in form or in spirit, we will always find home in the power of our trine.

We shed bittersweet tears during our good-bye. It was a new chapter of our relationship. And a new season of my life.

Holly and I had no doubt that while you were living Dad's dream, you would also discover and manifest your own.

•••

After you left, I started walking. With my dogs at my side, I walked. With firm and focused and furious footsteps, I walked. Day after day. Sometimes for hours at a time.

Movement was your meditation, Mom. It gave you clarity in the present and vision for the future.

"Ain't nothin' gonna break-a my stride, nobody gonna slow me down…"

Even the relentless bay wind couldn't break your stride!

The wind blew right through me, creating a hurricane across my inner landscape that I couldn't ignore. In its stir, I had no choice but to examine myself and my life in a way I had never done before.

You became passionate about discovering your purpose and cultivating your gifts. As a seeker committed to a path of expansion, you'd say, "Always remember, Nick, when you stop growing, you die."

Everyday I would wake up and ask, "How do I wish to learn Love today?" Inevitably, I would walk myself into an answer.

Your perseverance and perspective were inspiring, Mom.

I was ready to make my mark on the world. My pursuits were vast, from interior design projects to supporting children in unfortunate circumstances to advocacy for the arts.

Holly and I were amazed by the diversity of your days. We practically had to make an appointment to see you!

I was painting a new life for myself...a new landscape with with a whole new spectrum of color. I consulted with astrologers, psychics, and shamans to make meaning of my ever-expanding palate and my soul's evolution across time.

You were a mystic.

Til' the day I died, I never denied an opportunity to glean guidance from beyond...

You found your teacher in Cynthia Bischoff. Through her transformational Heartliving program, you discovered your heart language and your spiritual intelligence.

I have been a healer across many lifetimes. When I learned about energy work, a deep remembering came to Light. Receiving Reiki attunements from Cynthia woke me up to my innate abilities and reunited me with my sacred warrior archetype. Such an empowering gift!

For yourself...and for the people and animals on whom you laid your beautiful hands.

I could have done more with this gift. But there were other life assignments that called for my attention. Unlike healing, focus did not come naturally. In the autumn of my life, I found it difficult to attend to just one color, one interest at a time.

In one of your journals, I found your prayer...

"Please, Spirit. Help me to focus. Set my vibration on high so that I can recognize the awareness I need...for myself and all those I love."

Like so many, I received the blessing of your prayer, Mom. Realizing that my challenges stemmed from a source beyond my form, you set me on my own healing and awakening path.

It's why you came back this time around...to me.

Thank you, Mom, for initiating my journey to Truth.

•••

While your attention was dispersed, your focus never swayed from your family and your friends. Your passion for people was enduring.

I had a lifelong career in relationships. My family, of course, was my most important job...but I did a lot of moonlighting with my friends.

You were either on the phone—listening to, laughing with, and loving up the lucky one on the other end of the line—or you were writing one of your inspirational notes inside of a greeting card.

I was a connector of the head and the heart, for sure. I was also a channel through which people came together.

If there was a scene that best reflected your life, it would be the party, the absolute manifestation of your ability to gather, to beautify, and to enchant. You were an alchemist of entertainment!

Your dad and I were party artists. Together, we created sophisticated settings with soft lighting, decadent hors d'oeuvres, overflowing cocktails...and music that inspired everyone to shake their things! No one ever needed a dance floor to dance at our parties!

There was confidence and ease in your banter with everyone who walked through your door. With a tray of stuffed mushrooms resting on your arm, you'd meander through the crowd, leaving revelers awestruck by your sparkling charm.

I was a merrymaker and a mover. I found that when I stayed too long in a conversation at a social function, I said things I later regretted.

The party is the ultimate stage for human drama, which is magnified when alcohol is added to the scene.

And the script for the party often contains gossip about other people... Sometimes I'd find myself chiming in just to be part of the conversation.

As you started to wake up from the illusion of it all, you became keenly aware of the human tendency to criticize the other in the vain attempt to strengthen and protect the self. With this awareness and your commitment to Truth, you'd dance your way through parties, maintaining your authenticity and your status as the best hostess in town!

The older I got, the less tolerance I had for ego-driven conversations. I wanted to talk about what mattered. So I started asking people big questions about Life and Love...and listening deeply for their answers.

Remember the time you asked the woman who was fawning over Dad, "What exactly do you like about him?"

I really wanted to know. I wasn't angry or jealous, just profoundly curious.

I love you, Mom.

•••

Perhaps your grandchildren were the brightest Lights of your autumn. Each one added a unique color to the new life you were painting. We gave your first granddaughter your mom's name.

My Grace Alma.

You started working the fashion scene one day a week in Richmond, to get your city fix and your Grace fix. You'd spend the night with us every Wednesday.

Wednesdays with Nonie! I would send you and Mike out on dates so Grace and I had the space to remember each other. As an infant, she showed me the peace of stillness. She erased time for the hours we sat staring at each other. As she grew, it became obvious that she was a mover like me. We would stroll, and later walk hand in hand, all over town.

It was Grace who brought Holly home.

For many years, Holly needed to explore the world and herself, apart from us...but when she saw your curly-top baby, a combination of you and me as little ones, she couldn't resist the pull of her roots.

She left Seattle and landed in Richmond just in time to babysit Grace while Mike and I worked on conceiving Viv. With a box of donuts, I dropped Grace at Holly's apartment on one of her first days back in town. "Give me forty-five minutes," I said.

Oh, Nicki. It's a wonder she didn't head right back to the airport!

We had her, Mom. She wasn't going anywhere.

That was one of the most joyous times of my life. I had both my daughters in one place, a growing family, a stunning home on the water, and bountiful opportunities to give and grow in my own community. I was full. Perhaps fuller than I'd ever been in my life. My autumn color was at its peak!

When new friends met you during this time, they would exclaim, "Wow, your mom is beautiful!" And Mike's buddies had plenty to say about you too… "Hey man," Mike would rebuke, "that's my mom you're talking about!"

Beauty is just a reflection of happiness. And I was happy. As a proud matriarch, I was determined to live a long time, to witness the unfolding of this family I started. I was committed to taking care of myself, to staying young, to staying here…

With us.

My morning routine was intentional, guided by the mantra, "Breathe, Nourish, Love." It included a long walk, twenty minutes on the rebounder, lemon water and a spoonful of vinegar, a vast and ever-changing array of supplements, a phone call to a friend or a daughter, and a quick meditation filled with gratitude and white Light. I could never sit for long!

You'd bounce from your cushion to your closet to orchestrate the perfect outfit for the day, the outfit that would best reflect the current state of your inner-artist. You taught Holly and me to wear what makes us feel good. "Because when you feel good, you look good," you'd say. Thank you for giving me license to wear pigtails and flower-embroidered boots for the rest of my life…

You need no permission to love yourself, honey. Spirit gave you one form as your vehicle through this lifetime. Caring for it in all of its expressions is your responsibility. As I got older, my calendar was full of meetings and appointments that nurtured me mentally, emotionally, spiritually… and physically. Your dad would roll his eyes as I headed out for another facial or "a cut and color." I think we've already discussed the importance of hair.

Hair is power!

And don't you forget it!

With your radiant skin, your shiny locks, and your dazzling smile, you'd hit the streets of your world, illuminating any darkness that crossed your path.

The world was my classroom. And I stayed open to whatever experience presented itself to me.

You rarely talked about your random acts of kindness, Mom. But I know they were countless.

Life is as serendipitous as you allow it to be. The Love I experienced with friends, as well as with strangers, was between us...and the Divine.

Love was your language...kindness was your work.

•••

As I discovered my many layers, I realized my longing to share my wisdom and to speak my truth. But there was hesitation in my voice.

In a bold act of courage, you signed up for a public speaking course. In the end, you told your story and inspired the audience with your Light. Holly brought Grace to the main event so that she could witness her Nonie—as more than just her Nonie—as a woman in command. And you delivered, Mama.

Since the first grade, I had been insecure about the choice and flow of my words. This experience helped me realize that what I said was less important than how I made people feel. And, just by showing up authentically, I could make people feel...

With this awareness, you showed off your powerful skills as the director and host of the Allie Awards, a yearly event that honors artists of all genres for their achievements in the local community.

This was a big leap of faith for me. At board meetings, I would chant affirmations under my breath before putting my ideas on the table I feared would swallow me whole.

The board meeting is not our scene, Mom.

Stepping into a leadership role was totally outside of my comfort zone. Yet it was a call to combine my passion for the arts, my natural ability for event planning, and my desire to use my voice.

We all came to see you in your glory, Mom. A picture of grace and confidence, you were glowing on that stage.

I was a wreck of nerves, but I loved the spotlight...and it loved me. First-grade Nancy was redeemed and healed.

The applause for her, for you, was long overdue! I can still hear its echo.

Me too, honey.

•••

As I stepped more firmly into my power, I began to expand beyond the walls of my lovely home, beyond the gates of my neighborhood. I felt a yearning for more space, for my own space.

You were the glue of our family, Mom. And glue not only holds the pieces together, it also sets itself in place. This expansion was contrary to your adhesive nature.

As much as I cherished being in place, in togetherness with your dad and my family, there was a part of me that desperately wanted to break free. I had gone from my childhood home to my marital home—and after over fifty years of sharing walls, I craved a taste of freedom...a little retreat away from home, for a night or two a week.

You started apartment hunting in Richmond.

Just the exploration, the fantasy of my own little fort was liberating. But something held me back from actually manifesting my vision.

The glue.

Super glue, perhaps. Your dad was supportive of my venture, but also confused by it. I didn't want to cause him pain. I didn't want to make a mess. So I put my dream to rest...a choice I don't regret.

Our choices reveal our deepest truths.

The tension I felt was simply a conflict of my values—how could I hold commitment and freedom at once? Given the choice, I would always pick my people. My needs were not worth hurting those I loved. And having my own place would have hurt your dad...and weakened the glue that held us all together.

Instead of changing your circumstances, you changed your perspective.

As I started to hold your father and our life together more tenderly, I transformed MY dream for space into OUR dream for space.

You created a vision board, that sits in my family room today. It contains a lifetime of your precious memories and a pure projection of your future—all against the backdrop of a whimsical old tree, perhaps a foreshadowing of your Oakley. At the tree's roots are images of your roots—your childhood, your parents and grandparents. Rising up the trunk are reflections of family and the Love you cultivated with your children and grandchildren. The branches hold your wisdom, your beauty, your sense of adventure, your affirmation of Life and all it has to teach. And at the tippy top of the old oak tree is your invitation to possibility—the open hands and open road, the wild horses, the cabin in the mountains, the ever-burning candle.

The future I envisioned was about all of us—a space that we could all call home. A space to bring people and animals together, for learning and sanctuary. A space that would stay in our family long after this little life of mine. A space of purpose...

And you found this space, Mom.

Through my prayers, the space, the tree really, found me.

•••

Your dad and I went away for a couple nights to the foothills of Virginia. A change of scenery is a sure way to revive a sleepy marriage. Dad and I thrived when on retreat together. Away from routine and to-do lists, where we could remember each other and our Love.

You were the best teacher of perseverance through the ebbs and flows of marriage.

Marriage is hard work. And it can be the most meaningful work for the soul.

It was a testament to your amplified life force, Mom, that Dad came to embrace your dream of a home amongst the trees. I didn't think he could be pulled from the sirens of the sea.

I have my ways, honey...and your dad was ready to transcend the gated community for the open countryside...

It was your next horizon.

We were sitting in a coffee shop, browsing through a local magazine. In it was a notice of a farm house for sale, in an area we had never heard of before.

Scottsville.

As I looked at the photograph of this house, every cell in my body was alight. Even the name of the farm, Idylwood, resonated in the deepest part of me.

Like a song you'd been waiting to sing your whole life.

Dad called the agent, and even though she wasn't available, we drove out to Idylwood anyway.

And you saw Oakley.

Honey, when I met Oakley, it was like being welcomed home. Before I even looked at the the house, I knew this was the place I would live for the rest of this life...

A holy moment. A merging of soul and spirit.

Oakley was the answer to my prayer, inviting me into the future I'd envisioned. My heart opened and I could feel myself breaking free into this expansive space of creativity. The land of Idylwood vibrated with purpose.

And on it, you vibrated with purpose. I found your affirmation in your journal...

"I am a temple of Light that will connect everything with joy. I will be happy and share..."

My vision was clear. There would be circles and classes here. There would be learning and healing here. There would be a growing family here. There would be unyielding Love here.

And there would be a deepening of your relationship with Dad here.

We were strongest when planning and building together, when looking out in the same direction...

While you were renovating the house, renovating your life, you always answered the phone laughing.

I was happy. I was free. I was home.

●●●

The summer you moved to Idylwood, I turned forty. And I had a vision of my own.

Yes, you did, baby girl. Just in front of Oakley, there was an empty patch of land surrounded by a ring of boxwoods. It was asking to be transformed.

It was asking for a labyrinth.

What a perfect birthday gift for you and a rebirthday gift for Idylwood.

The labyrinth is a moving metaphor—a hero's journey into the center of the soul...and a return to the world with a more profound sense of Truth.

It's a symbol for how I lived and how you are continuing to live your Life. The spiritual journey is not measured in miles, but in moments, in which we remember that there is nowhere to go...

We are already here.

Walking my neighborhood labyrinth, sometimes one inch at a time, helped me remember, Mom. One morning I entered with an intention to release the dark thoughts that had been tormenting me. Through the twists and turns of the passage, I rested in the tender kiss of the breeze and the golden warmth of the sun. As I gave thanks for the return of my Light, I noticed I was not alone. There beside me, dark and mysterious and ever-present in the Truth, was my shadow.

When we stand in the Truth of non-duality, we see that the shadow is nothing to fear. It is simply part of the Light.

When I reached the final turn of my meditation that day, I invited my shadow to re-enter the world with me. Without resistance, I allowed the tormenting thoughts to create a wildfire of Light, to inflame and burn through me…until all that was left of my story was ash. For an eternal moment, I was free.

The labyrinth had to be built. For you, for our family, for Idylwood, for Truth.

My dear husband of all trades designed a simple labyrinth and collected the stones and supplies to build it. With family and best friends, we laid each stone to create this memorial to Truth. And we walked it together, a journey into our tribal soul.

Oakley watched over us.

As he does every time we place our feet on this sacred path.

Many feet have walked this path.

It was an integral part of our women's circle.

How grateful I was for our circle, honey, my vision for Idylwood manifested. Guided by ritual and the wisdom of the moon, we held space for women to explore and share their own wisdom, their own Light.

It was a co-creation of magic, Mama. To culminate each circle, we walked the labyrinth by the Light of our candles and the moon…passing each other on our individual journeys, touching hands and remembering our Divine feminine bond.

We stopped meeting when I got sick. I grieved for this loss, but the foundation had been laid. There would be more circles, more learning, more Love on this land. It was just the beginning of possibility.

About four months after you crossed over, Holly and I invited our circle to gather again in your honor. A bowl of your ashes was our centerpiece. To close, we walked the labyrinth. In the center, the place of illumination, we held your ashes in the palm of our hands. We felt your timeless essence and then offered you back to the Earth. Some of you was scattered by Oakley, some on the coats of your beloved four-leggeds, but most landed on the path of our labyrinth...

...where you will always remember me as the Earth on which you walk your Truth. A spiral of questions and answers...and space for silence. Just like this book, our labyrinth on paper.

•••

There was a shadow around your commitment to staying young, Mom.

Yes, there was, honey. I was attached to my identity as a beautiful and busy woman. Western medicine offered the promise of prolonged youth and sustained energy in a synthetic hormone replacement therapy that not only perpetuated a false belief, but a harmful one. I knew this was a dangerous road, but I took it anyway. My ego was louder than my intuition.

You were holding on tight to your vibrant leaves, Mom. You didn't know that by letting go, you would meet an expansive beauty beyond your youth.

I was caught in the illusion that my appearance and my purpose-driven life were proof of my significance, my worthiness. Slowing down to honor the falling of my leaves was not an option.

Nothin' gonna break your stride...

I would not surrender my identity to menopause. Regardless of the risk, I would hold on to my story for as long as possible.

No human can say what caused the cancer, Mom. As beings on this polluted planet, we are susceptible to an array of harmful toxins. But you took such care in caring for yourself, in protecting yourself from negative external influences. Your choice to submit to artificial hormones was a detour that may very well have cost you your life.

It's true, honey.

This detour was proof of the damage the ego can cause. The danger of identity. But even in your missteps, you were my teacher, Mom.

It was part of our Divine play...

Right after you passed, your teacher Cynthia said to me, "A mother's passing is her daughter's passage." And while I didn't understand it at the time, I allowed it to be a mantra of my heart.

My passing would embolden you to explore other portals, beyond your identity as form.

I quit teaching. It was the first step in the exploration of who I really am. If I'm not a teacher, who am I?

Over time, you would learn to rest in the unknown. You would discover the nothingness that contains everything...the ordinary that is extraordinary.

•••

As usual, my mind was way ahead of my spirit on this journey. My ego was still in control when I changed my status on Linkedin (an employment-oriented social networking service) from teacher to human being. Consumed by my desire to understand the art of being, I read and wrote obsessively about spirituality in form and even published some articles on awakening.

But your expressions were still products of the mind, not yet embodied Truths.

I clung to the external validation I received as proof of my significance in the world. If I wasn't a teacher, I was a spiritual writer. And if I wasn't writing, I was meditating or creating sacred ceremony.

While you had transformed your identity, it was still an identity. No matter how spiritual the action—where there is pride, there is ego. But the more conscious part of you knew to continue asking the questions...

If I'm not a writer, who am I? If I'm not a mother, wife, sister, friend, who am I? If I'm not a human being, as I so boldly announced on Linkedin, who am I?

And you found the Divinity in...nothing.

•••

It's easy to stay awake to the Truth when playing with words behind my computer screen, meditating on my cushion in the solace of my backyard, or sitting in a circle with like-hearted souls.

These are worthy endeavors, honey, but Life wants you to bring the spirit of wonder and Oneness into the world at large.

Unlike the perfect shape and clear agenda of the circle, the world is random and wild, a geometric mess of human stuff—opinions, fears, gifts, roles, personality traits—all mixing together in a way that ultimately triggers my need for control.

And your ego is all too willing to swoop in and lead you back to your prison cell of separation consciousness. All in the name of keeping the little you safe.

A ruthless jailer, the ego spins endless commentary that loops in the background of my interactions with others—revealing the density of my human conditioning, the duality of my thoughts, my attachment to identity, my need to be validated.

Here is a clip, perhaps a bit exaggerated, of my ego at work...

"My nose is huge compared to hers. I'm ugly."
"I do have a nice bottom. I'm pretty cute."
"I have nothing to offer to this conversation. I'm stupid."
"That was a wickedly wise thing to say. I'm smart."
"She is so successful. What do I have to show for my life? I'm insignificant."
"They are impressed that I'm writing a book and that I once modeled underwear. I'm special."
"Why do I have to be so serious, so heavy? I am a real downer."
"They liked my joke. I am really funny."
"Nobody is talking to me. Nobody likes me."

"I am really popular tonight. Everybody likes me."
"He has bad breath."
"Do I have bad breath?"
"Why am I here? I want to go home!"

It's easy to get sucked back into the trance, into the false beliefs of mind that keep us separated from each other and the present moment. When we live in this illusion, we suffer.

Because even when the ego is all puffed up, parading around the cell, high on the affirmation it received for being *good* in some way, it is just a matter of time before Life offers an experience that elicits the opposite response. And the ego finds itself curled up in the fetal position in the corner of the cell, believing it's *bad* in some way…

Life is your teacher, honey. It will continue to present dynamics that allow you to see when your ego is in charge…until you finally realize that any thought that creates division is untrue.

We are not our thoughts or our points of view—we are the space behind our thinking minds.

Engaging with others from this space is the key to thriving in the world. Look for the face of the Divine in each of your fellow travelers, and remember that they, too, are shackled by their own little thoughts. They, too, are struggling to navigate the messy landscape of the world. There is nothing to want or prove or seek, honey. There is just being with whatever unfolds in each moment…and relaxing in the Truth of it.

I'm learning, Mom. I've come a long way from believing my ego's commentary. When I catch a glimpse of absolute reality, where there is no good or bad, right or wrong, I can feel just how extraordinary the ordinary is.

Like every other form on this planet, you are an ordinary masterpiece.

Recently, I was at a party and found myself in a conversation with a fellow who wanted to tell me all about his guinea pigs. While he was very excited about this topic, I was bored out of my mind. I made an awkward exit to the bathroom, where I found some peace…and some tweezers to pluck my eyebrows.

You were in judgement, honey. What we think about someone else sometimes says more about us than them. What if you had chosen fascination over criticism of this human experience? What if you had simply noticed and been present with the unique way Spirit was manifesting through this human?

I would have softened and transformed my contraction into expansion. Maybe those guinea pigs had some kind of message for me, something I needed to learn…if I had only opened to the possibility that a connection would reveal itself.

And maybe there was no message at all. Yet the conversation was happening within that moment. And that moment was all you had. Might as well have leaned in…

…and danced with the ordinary miracle of it.

I hope you start to dance more, honey. Life wants to be your partner. Your eyebrows can wait.

•••

I am dancing, Mom… Every Sunday I arrive in my body for the dance of 5Rhythms. The founder of this amazing practice, Gabrielle Roth, looks like you. Her spirit is present in every class…as is yours.

I am dancing with you, honey.

I begin with the rhythm of *flowing*, a feminine surrender to my feet, trusting they will take me where I need to go. I celebrate the sensation of gliding, sauntering, skipping across the floor. From *flowing*, I transition to the rhythm of *staccato*, tapping into my masculine warrior energy, my personal boundaries, my heartbeat. I remember my exhale and my unique expression of self before I am propelled into the rhythm of *chaos*. Wild and creative, I am out of my mind, moving faster than thought, like a raging river. I find ease in the madness and I embrace the discord. Exhilarated and inspired, I step into the rhythm of *lyrical*, reconnected to my patterns and cycles and the form I inhabit. I explore my relationship with other dancers and accept whatever is revealed. Are my eyes open or closed to other? Am I playful or shy? Finally, I dissolve into the rhythm of *stillness*, cradling the wisdom of my body. I meet Spirit. I meet you.

You meet Truth.

One Sunday, my teacher Samantha shared the analogy of movement as a way to escape the cage of our existence. The cage door is always open, she said, but we often stay imprisoned, because we forget that we are free.

Humans forget.

Through the portal of music and Samantha's poetic guidance, I could feel myself grasping the unlocked door of my cage, holding it shut, fearing the unknown on the others side of it. My body was not a vehicle of liberation, but the cage itself. I was frozen. As the music reverberated in my chest, I shook myself silly in an effort to release my spirit, but I couldn't shake the density of my flesh. I felt heavy and discouraged and trapped by my mind's refusal to surrender to the freedom that was right there waiting for me. I became still and heard your voice.

You are holding on so tightly to your soul stories, honey...the beautiful ones and the ugly ones. But no story is who you are. Your obsession with thoughts and words and images are leading you away from the Truth. Let go of your struggle to understand. Lay down the stories, the memories that live in your cells. And live in this moment. Feel yourself as the big sky and the small bird that flies fearlessly into the mystery.

And so I allowed my body to move again, this time with ease and grace...orbiting other dancers who were also freeing themselves from their cages and dissolving into the unknown.

The stories flew from the cage of my heart like birds. And I transformed from human to hawk—I was the body and you were the wings. We soared across the realms of reality and into the Truth of existence. I was majestic, exhilarated, and free...for a moment.

After class, as I stepped back out into the expanse of the world, I heard you like a poem on the wind...

Oh sweet thing,
The Earth is your dance floor,
Welcoming your rhythmic joy and sorrow,
Enduring the pounding of your feet and fists,
Reminding you of your wings.
Dance your soul clean, little bird,

And then take flight
Across nothing and everything.
Surrender, sweet thing,
To the wonder of Life.

And a bluebird flew by...

"Zip-a-dee-doo-dah, zip-a-dee-ay...my, oh my, what a wonderful day..."

•••

On your birthday, I invited you to join me on a shamanic journey.

And I accepted.

You always gave Holly and me presents on your birthday.

I loved giving presents.

You still do. I met you in the realm of Spirit with your elephant...

A symbol of my commitment to you and your sister...and to uncovering
my own wisdom.

And your horse...

My power and freedom.

I traveled with my giraffe, my intuition and my connection between
Heaven and Earth.

I took you to a waterfall and presented you with a magical mirror.

As I drank in my reflection, I heard your Divine message in the rush of
falling water.

You are... all of it.

And at once, in the mirror, I was all of it. Victim and villain. Good and
bad. Right and wrong. I was duality in form.

Now, release it all...

The stories of lifetimes burned through me. The terror, the rage, the anguish... a flood of fire. I stood under the waterfall, baptizing myself in the cool surge of your voice...

There is nothing to fear.

You blessed my path of healing and awakening.

And there was more. A glimpse of Heaven for my baby girl on my birthday and her rebirthday.

You led me into bliss, for what seemed like a moment and forever.

Happy Birthday...to us.

•••

I've joined an "Awakening the Warrior" storytelling circle.

Your sister's gift to you.

In your physical absence, she continues to lead me back to myself, reminding me of the gift of being in human form...

It was her unspoken promise to me.

The facilitator of this circle, the amazing Leah Lamb, downloaded a story from the Universe about a woman's meeting with Venus. It was not a warm and fuzzy encounter. Venus, the quintessential archetype of the Divine feminine, laughed in the woman's face. And in response, the woman's heart actually left her body and moved toward different aspects of herself—aspects that manifested as the blue butterfly, the bear, the crocodile, and the hummingbird.

Images of the Goddess herself.

As I tapped into my connection with these animals, my heart met the butterfly with easeful familiarity, in a place of Spirit and expansion. We were old friends. The bear aroused the sleeping bear in me...the embodiment of my power, my commitment to the Earth. The hummingbird was welcoming, but elusive. How does she sustain her joy? Oh, how I long for it!

The hummingbird is in you, honey. She's just quiet right now. Resting.

I've been carrying a picture of two-year-old Nicki on her Big Wheel tricycle, in the fullness of her joy. My inner hummingbird is waking up, slowly...

And the crocodile?

It barely acknowledged me, which was just fine with me. I had absolutely no desire to connect with this creature or to explore its offerings.

What does the crocodile represent to you?

The most asleep part of my warrior. The part that doesn't have to explain herself. The part that doesn't have to apologize for herself. The part that isn't afraid to say "F--- you."

Ah, that part.

I was riding home with Mike last night. And he was driving how he drives.

Aggressively, but skillfully.

While he has a gift for maneuvering through dense traffic, he's always a little too close, for my comfort, to the car in front of him.

He drives without hesitation, much like he lives.

So last night, as we were headed home from a lovely date, he had to slam on breaks because, in my opinion, he was once again riding the bumper of the car ahead of us. And the argument we've had a million times before rose yet again. But this time, I actually told him to F--- off.

Oh boy.

And it felt so good!

I bet it did.

He didn't deserve it. It was probably unfair to unleash my wrath on him. But it had to be said.

You've never said that to anyone before?

Not out loud. And for the first time ever in any relationship, I had no desire to apologize or to explain myself for my behavior or my words.

You were the crocodile.

And owning that part of myself is essential for my awakening in this lifetime.

It's the ultimate antidote to our "Just be nice" family mantra.

Grandma is probably shaking her head...

No, Grandma is applauding your moxie...and your willingness to examine every aspect of yourself.

There are parts of us that aren't pretty, that are quite savage, in fact. Yet they are just as Divine as the pleasant parts of us, perhaps even more so.

You are embracing your wholeness, honey. I love you so much.

I love me too, crocodile and all!

•••

Eleven months after you passed, for Holly's fiftieth birthday, we decided to get tattoos. We wanted your signature on our physical forms. We wanted to wear you permanently.

Nothing is permanent, honey, except Love.

As Holly and I waited to have our skin branded in your honor, my mind wandered back in time to another story of a tattoo...

It was an unintentional branding from a car accident seven years earlier, in which the force of the airbag left a burn—in the shape of a giraffe—on the inside of my wrist. The accident was my fault. It was my worst fear come true. I hurt a lady and her three children, not seriously, but enough to fuel in me an ancient and toxic guilt.

I wrote a letter to the victim, named Wanda, offering my sincerest apologies for causing harm to her and her family. My sister delivered it, along with a bouquet of flowers.

After her visit, Holly called me in tears and said, "Nick, Wanda was beyond gracious and forgiving. Honey, she reminded me of you." Wanda was an African-American single mom, unemployed and struggling to make ends meet. But her spirit transcended her circumstances. "She was pure and beautiful—and human," Holly said, "just like you, just like all of us."

As my sister spoke, I exhaled into the Truth that was bigger than this one little experience, this one little lifetime.

The following month, I went to court, ready to declare my guilt, to receive my punishment, to balance my karma. My friend Ed, a lawyer, was with me for support. "Let me do the talking," he said, well aware of my compulsion to crucify myself. As we waited to be called, I noticed a familiar face a few rows in front of us. It was Wanda.

Against Ed's advice, I went to sit beside her. We looked into each other's misty brown eyes as if we had known each other for lifetimes. There was much to say, but we were warned twice by the bailiff to be quiet. So we just held hands in silence.

When it was our turn, Wanda and I approached the bench, arm in arm. Ed followed behind, shaking his head in disbelief. "Judge, in all my years practicing law, I've never witnessed this before. I think I'll let the victim speak first."

Wanda told the judge that she was there to testify to my innocence. She said she saw me look both ways before crossing her path—that this was truly an accident, the result of a blind spot and a dangerous intersection… and that she and her children were fine.

The judge looked at Ed and smiled, "I don't think I've ever witnessed this either… Case dismissed!"

Wanda and I hugged each other and then we hugged Ed. We would have hugged the judge and the bailiff too, but we restrained ourselves. I'd like to think that everyone in courtroom was cheering from their heart space. In one miraculous moment, Wanda illuminated the blind spots of duality in the courtroom, in our culture, in our world. She and I did not stand before the judge as black and white, poor and privileged, innocent and guilty. Wanda had built a bridge, on which we stood as pure Spirit in form, united far beyond our stories of this lifetime.

As I left the courthouse that day, I looked at the giraffe on the inside of my wrist and heard its message: "You are of Earth and Heaven. Be gentle with yourself and your fellow travelers. Life is full of blind spots. Illuminate them."

Thank you, Giraffe. Thank you, Wanda. Thank you, Life.

•••

Back at the tattoo parlor, I realized that the giraffe on the inside of my wrist had completely faded. After seven years, I no longer needed the daily reminder of the giraffe's message. I had received and embodied it. Now, in the very same place on my wrist, I wanted the daily reminder of you.

So you chose a tattoo artist with the last name Pease.

For Holly's birthday, this had to be a sacred experience. Certainly, with a last name like Pease, this artist would deliver what we desired.

Did he?

Well, when he came to the lobby to meet us, the first thing we noticed was his t-shirt. It said, "The Pussyfier." I tried not to take in the image accompanying the label. Holly and I exchanged defeated glances and shuffled back to his studio. We brought candles and stones and a picture of you to create the scene of this spiritual event that we would share with the pussyfier.

Could you hear my laughter?

We heard you, Mom. Heavy with grief, we needed your laughter to lighten us. I squeezed Holly's hand as the pussyfier punctured and pigmented the delicate skin of my wrist with your signature.

Love…Me

The only words that mattered in the world. Thank you, Mr. Pease. You delivered.

•••

As my eyes began to open to the illusion and confusion of it all, my path became clear.

Tracey—our teacher, healer, and friend—was your guide.

She encouraged me to sign up for a VortexHealing® Divine Energy Healing class, a class I had already taken two years earlier...

...before you were ready to step out of the world of doing and into the world of being, before you were ready to trust Life and trust yourself.

Now I was ready. To deeply explore this healing and awakening path. To receive personal transmissions from Merlin, the avatar of of this lineage of Divine energy and consciousness. To devote myself to magical transformation through this wheel of spinning Light in my heart.

Another circle of Light.

This time I was open to whatever Merlin had to show me...until he shifted my relationship with you.

It had to be done, honey.

In a lucid dream, I killed the false part of myself...and left her in a bathtub.

Well, we do love our bathtubs.

This isn't funny, Mom.

Oh, but it is! Lighten, Nicki Beans.

So, Divine forces, dressed as policemen and carrying Nerf guns, came to take me away for this act of Truth, to escort me from the bathroom, the prison cell of my ego, into a deeper layer of my being.

This is delightful, honey!

This is serious, Mom! I slammed the door on all-powerful police. "I will not leave little me in the bathtub!" I screamed.

Behind the toilet, I found a police uniform and a Nerf gun, a costume that would allow me to play the role of an awakened being without having to surrender any piece of my identity.

A classic spiritual bypass…but your facade did not fool the Divine forces.

The police swarmed the bathroom, stripped me of my disguise, and led me to you, sitting on the brown and orange plaid sofa in our old living room. Through tears, you said to me,

"Go in peace, honey…"

"No," I argued, "not without you…"

So I held your hand and we walked with the Nerf gun-armed policemen through a magical mist that contained everything and nothing at once…

The next day in class, the teacher used her Vortex magic to dissolve the issue realm most obscuring my lens on Life. Merlin showed me the predominant role I played to protect my little self, to hide from Truth. He showed me the child who desperately needed her mother.

This dynamic was the main theme of our Divine play in this lifetime.

Even as an adult, I was the insecure child who sought constant approval and reassurance from you…and the rest of the world that, over time and in various ways, represented you.

That's powerful insight, honey, and with insight comes change.

Over the next few days, I was furious with you. I bagged up some of your precious things and carelessly tossed them in a charity bin. I ripped down the sticky notes that bordered my mirror— the messages from you that validated me, us—what I thought was Truth. I didn't want to hear your voice. I even considered deleting our book.

Without the identity of the needy child, who was I?

You were awareness…slowly waking up to the hollow and hallowed wholeness of you.

Yes, slowly…

After burning through my rage, I gained some clarity. I realized that shifting my definition of Love was the first step on this new path. While Love might include a conscious exchange of validation and praise, it is not defined by conditions of any sort. True love is unattached and free.

And it starts with the Love of self.

I have to take you off the pedestal, Mom.

I never wanted to be on the pedestal, honey.

I know. But I needed you there.

And now you don't. These pages are full of your innate wisdom. You don't need me to show you the way. You are the way. The tears I shed in your dream were symbolic of your release into this Truth. Holding your hand through the magical mist was the final scene of our old movie.

And now we need no movie… We have become the screen.

We are beyond the roles of mother and daughter, teacher and learner. We are just two souls doing our work, finding the Truth layer by layer.

You are more than my mother for a short lifetime. You are the part of my consciousness that is allowing me to rebirth myself.

You wouldn't have followed this path if I were still in form.

No.

A mother's passing is her daughter's passage.

•••

Without you here in form, Mom, Holly and I are learning to navigate our relationship as sisters without a mother. You raised us to love one another unconditionally. And if there was conflict, you were the bridge between our differences. Maintaining the power and purity of our trine was your Life's work.

I am still the bridge between you, and our trine is still strong. Home is us, honey. Yet now is the time for you and your sister to see each other as individuated women, beyond your roles as my daughters, beyond the dynamic of your sisterhood.

I've been doing some deep inquiry and healing work around this, Mom. Sisterhood provides some of the most fertile ground for soul growth. I know you so wanted to cultivate this ground with your own sister.

There were many seeds planted in the earth of my relationship with Joy. But they never came to flower. Neither of us cared for the soil as tenderly as we could have. Neither of us were willing to get our hands dirty with the discomfort of our differences, the Truth of our pain. I'm doing the work for both of us now. I'm glad you are doing it with your sister while still in human form.

Me too, Mom. It's fascinating to see how Life plays through us, how our soul covenants are unfolding and intersecting.

You've been each other's greatest teachers since the beginning.

As a young child with an unyielding appetite for affection, I never felt full.

Oh, I remember.

So I looked to my big sister—who was independent, adventurous, and bold—and decided that she was the answer to the wholeness I was seeking.

You copied everything she did.

If I could be her, I reasoned, then I would be full. And over time, while I certainly developed my own identity, I never outgrew the belief that Holly's way was the best way. I coveted her charm, her effervescence, her eloquence. In my young adulthood, I developed a fierce jealousy of my sister, that I covered with an artificial light. This was exacerbated by your pride in and praise of us, Mom. For me, it created an unhealthy level of competition with Holly. Whoever was the most special in your eyes, I believed, was also the most loved. And your love was all this needy child ever wanted.

On your healing path, you allowed the jealousy you had suppressed to surface. In all its ugliness. In all its beautiful Truth.

Holly was the drum I wanted to be.

Until you realized that you are the chime...and your sound is equally as potent.

While I honor Holly's drum, it can overpower me sometimes. I've needed space away from her to explore this lifetime dynamic and to learn to stand on my own, apart from our trine.

As you've exposed the illusion of your identity, you've dismantled your false belief that anyone is more special than another.

Just like I had to take you off the pedestal, I had to do the same with my sister.

Holly is a force of Love. She has the idealism of a child and the will of a warrior. And while this can be overwhelming for you, it is also a gift. She is teaching you to stand more firmly in your own Truth. To make your chime heard. She is listening, honey.

I know, Mom. And the force of my emotions is overwhelming for her. But she honors my need to express myself, even when she doesn't understand me. Even when I don't understand myself. We are learning to make music together, experimenting with different instruments, resting in the rests of our songs.

I'll always meet you there.

There has been some disharmony in our grieving, as we hold you in different Light at different times. Holly says you are her one true Love and she speaks your name like a prayer. And I feel as if I've absorbed you, rarely needing to speak of you as a separate form.

The energy that connects the three of us may vibrate differently. But it is all born of Spirit. A Love bigger than the mind can imagine.

For Grace's eighteenth birthday, she and I got matching tattoos. Two overlapping triangles—two trines representing the bond between her grandmother, her aunt, and her mother…and the bond between her mother, her sister, and herself.

The power of family. The power of women. The power of Love.

•••

Let's talk about sex, Mom. Every good book has a little sex in it!

Oh dear. Didn't we have this talk about thirty-five years ago?

I think it's time, in this season of my life and in your afterlife, that we revisit and revise that talk. Since I've burned through much my karmic guilt and shame around sex, I now have some space to really explore the beauty of it. You were so private about this part of your life, Mom, even when Holly and I were adults. It's time you come clean!

Some of my inhibition was a symptom of my attachment to the "nice girl" identity. Nice girls didn't talk about sex in my day. And certainly not in my parents' house. If it wasn't nice, we didn't talk about it.

Sex is pretty nice, Mom.

Oh Nicki, you know what I mean.

I can feel you blushing, Mom! Or is that me?

When Holly was a teenager, she asked me if I was a virgin when I married your father.

Your response?

I told her it was none of her business, which, from my perspective at the time, was true—and not entirely a reflection of my inner nice girl. While this was a dominant aspect of my character, I was also very much a woman of mystery.

You liked to keep certain pieces of yourself…for yourself.

And I had two daughters who incarnated with a zest for sharing everything! Your free-spirited sister reveled in her sensual nature and

188

delighted in telling stories with high shock value... and you compulsively confessed to what you considered your sins of the flesh—as well as the sins of the world, which you claimed as your own. I tried to meet both you and your sister in your raw disclosures, while still maintaining my own privacy.

You told us that sex was a beautiful exchange of Love between people who are committed to each other. You didn't specify that *those people* should be married, but that's how I heard you. It felt like an unspoken family pact.

I just wanted you to be ready. Your emotional vulnerability concerned me. I wish I had been more forthright in our sex talk.

Remember the drive to my first gynecologist appointment? You insisted on taking me, and the tension in the car was thick.

I didn't want to ask you directly if you were having sex with your boyfriend...

So instead you told me that the doctor would be asking if I was having sex with my boyfriend.

You remained silent for minutes. And when I couldn't stand it any longer, I pushed, 'Well, what are you going to say?'

After a long pause, I said, 'Sometimes?'

Like it was a question! I responded with my fiery temper.

The guilt and shame around premarital sex had already been triggered in me. And there was grief around my perceived loss of innocence, the corruption of my own "nice girl" image. Your reaction was just a mirror of my feelings.

In reality, I was less upset about the fact you were having sex—safely and with a boy you loved—than I was about the fact you didn't tell me. You, my baby who told me everything! This was new territory for us.

But all I could see was your disappointment.

I'm sorry, honey. I wish I had told you what is so clear to me now—that sex is a human birthright! It is part of the joy and ecstasy of being in form. And while it is best when intentional and genuine and in Love, it is also just plain fun—a Light-filled celebration of Life. Depriving oneself of such a gift, based on an archaic "nice girl" belief system, is a violence to the body... and to Life.

Listen to you! I hear you, Mom. After twenty-two years of marriage, I'm finally tapping into my inner Goddess...and the Divinity of my sexuality. Mike and I are enjoying our sensual explorations!

Good for you, honey. Spirit is cheering you on!

Remember the Magic Wand, Mom?

We're really going to write about this?

Yes. Let's hold nothing back!

When I started seeing Dr. Bush, he turned me on to—oh, that's a poor choice of words...

Perfect choice of words, Mom!

Oh dear. I am blushing now. You tell it.

He turned you on to a glorified vibrator designed to heal the body through pleasure.

There I was sitting in the doctor's office getting a tutorial on masturbation!

The nice girl and mystery woman took the back seat for this ride!

I felt so free. So empowered. This was for my health after all.

And *our* health—you bought Holly and me Magic Wands for Christmas! We added them to our respective collections. Mike calls this one my friend.

Oh Nicki.

I love my *friend*! And I love my Mama!

•••

I'm packing today for Ireland, Mom… Do you think I should take my *friend*?

Sure, honey. Why not?!

Mom! I'm finally going to Ireland—the trip my soul has been planning for lifetimes!

A solo adventure for my baby girl. You go, honey!

When I began my spiritual journey, I had a vision of myself sitting in a field of wildflowers. And surrounding me, on all sides, were green, rolling hills as far as the eye could see. This picturesque scene, that I somehow knew as Ireland, became a metaphor for my journey. The ups and downs, the mystery, the eternal nature of Life—animated by the natural beauty of this charmed place on Earth.

You never really claimed your German or English roots. For you, Ireland held the key to your heritage…and your heart.

I once tapped into a past life as a traveling storyteller in the Emerald Isle, a lifetime that followed one of horrific trauma—rape, torture, insanity, murder. Ireland offered me the space I needed to heal and rediscover human goodness. This gem of an island reawakened me to the magic and wonder of Life. It was what my soul needed then…

And it's what it needs now…a return to your fairy lineage.

I connected with my fairy essence in my thirties. And my resonance with the elemental world has grown over the last fifteen years. My fairy godmother, Terry, has taken me on journeys into the fairy realm that, in many ways, feels more like home than this dimension. In fairy form, I am lighter and freer and more joyful than I've ever been in human form.

The fairies have been calling you to Ireland for some time.

Grandma will join me there. She has fairy essence too, a discovery I made on one of my journeys across realms, when I landed beside the babbling brook in her backyard. As a child in this lifetime, I played with the elementals there.

A magical memory. A dream of dreams...

On this particular journey, a bluebird perched in a weeping willow tree, was there to greet me.

Somehow, I've always been wherever you are.

Across all time and space, Mom, you have been the bluebird on my shoulder.

I may have met Merlin in my grandparents' backyard too, although I first knew him as my guide named Shine.

Divinity shines through many forms, through many stories.

In this story, Merlin presented me with a star-studded, midnight-blue box. I opened it to find a void of golden, swirling Light, a portal to another dimension where I could connect with all beings in the galaxy...as I had done in past or perhaps parallel lives as a fairy.

You will rediscover the swirling Light in Ireland, honey. The fairies are waiting for you...as is the bluebird.

I'll look for you there, Mom.

•••

Ireland gave me the peace I've been searching for my whole life. In its pristine stillness and quiet, I found my breath...my fullness and my emptiness.

The boundless vista of sea, sky, and green Earth opened you to your own infinite nature.

The beauty was overwhelming. Wild daisies grew from moss-covered stones. Never a more perfect representation of you, Mom. Timeless strength giving birth to sweet purity.

Daisies are memorials of the Earth's innocence. And stones are her bones, supporting our healing and our growth. Rarely was my kitchen without a vase of daisies. And stones, of all shapes, colors, and sizes, were my companions through Life.

In your pockets and purses, on your side tables, and placed throughout your outdoor space, stones were your grounding and your guideposts for the journey.

I traveled with you through Ireland, honey...listening to the stones tell the stories of this enchanted land.

And what stories they told! Everything on my path was made of stone...from quaint cottages to castles, temples to towers. Stone circles and standing stones still pulse with the healing power with which they were placed centuries ago. I could feel you in their harmonic vibration, Mom.

We danced together in the circles, honey.

I could feel you in the animals too. Horses, cows, sheep, and donkeys roamed freely across the countryside, united with the land and its people. Ireland offered infinite space to get lost...and then found. Space to surrender completely.

Without limitation or fear. Like Heaven!

The rainbows were never-ending, born of my tears and your Light...

...and the magic of fairy.

The fairies found me, Mom! They revealed themselves on film as vibrant purple and blue and green orbs. Their Divine message was clear.

You were ready to hear it.

It was time to reconnect with my elemental energy. To, once and for all, lay down the mind-generated stories and the need to make meaning of my evolution.

As I sat on the verdant Irish hilltop, surrounded by the rolling terrain, I found myself within the original vision that initiated my spiritual journey. Yet I felt no need to explore the hills, the stories of my soul. I had no desire to examine the details—the who-what-when-where-why of me— across lifetimes. With the fairies and the fairy-human hybrids who so kindly took me under their wings, I began to rest in the spiral of Life...

...in the simultaneous nature of past, present, and future.

I met Gwen, a sister from another time and a flute maker who plays her melodies for the fairies in the hawthorn trees. Together, we toured the coast in her VW bus, swallowed by the surreal scenery of our dream. In the pouring rain, we walked along the Cliffs of Moher, hypnotized by the fog and fugue of the place...merged with the spirit of the dragon who lives there, merged with Life.

You were soaked to the bone, saturated with mystery...

...and surrendered to the only certainty available to humans. As I stood on those majestic cliffs, I realized that all I know for sure is that I was born and I will die.

Yes...and there is so much joy available to you in between, honey. You just have to choose it. Like Gwen. It's really quite simple.

Simple. Not always easy.

The path can be rocky. But you are better equipped than ever for the journey. The enchantment you experienced in Ireland is within you. Trust yourself, honey.

I trust Life, Mom. Thank you for giving it to me.

•••

The other day, someone asked Rhode what I've been doing for work since I left teaching. My fourteen-year-old man-child responded, "She's a spiritual person."

I love my grandson.

As I observed my reaction to his sweet acknowledgement, I recognized my residual attachment to identity. There was some pride, some desire to expand on his statement, to share the *doing* part of my *being*. But in my noticing, the desire dissolved.

The world will continue to entice you back into the illusion, into the separation consciousness of self-worth. Shining authentic Light on your internal experience of any occurrence will always illuminate the Truth.

As I more deeply embody the Truth of being human, I can feel the difference between being separate...and being autonomous.

As humans, we are designed with our own unique fragrance. This essence gives rise to our actions, to our individual contributions to the world.

In the Divine play of Life, our only responsibility is to assume the role presented to us in each moment...and then allow Spirit to shine through our form. It is only in this state of allowance that we can rise above the stage of human drama to see the web of connection we all share...

Autonomy without separation... I am because we are.

In the past, I put so much unnecessary effort toward being good, perfect, or special—all for the sake of feeling loved and safe in what I perceived as a dangerous world. Fear kept me separate and blinded to the Truth...

We are all just part of an energetic web, a cradle that holds us in unimaginable Love.

While I have not shed the density of my human flesh and taken flight with the fairies, I am feeling much freer on my journey through this lifetime. As I continue on the Vortex Healing path, my karmic load is lighter, my conditioned psychology is clearer, and the voice of my ego is softer.

You have taken huge leaps into the autumn of your life, honey. Your vibrant leaves are truer than ever...and you are more and more willing to let them go.

Like everyone else on the planet, I am a "spiritual person." And I'm rediscovering the joy of the hummingbird as I dabble in the world of human experience—delivering flowers, sorting trash and recycling at festivals, substitute teaching, playing with the words on these pages, and using my Love skills to perform various odd jobs.

You've got some pretty good Love skills, honey.

Thanks, Mom. I come by them naturally.

This is true.

As I am learning to take myself less seriously, I need less sleep. Spirit sometimes visits in the middle of the night to wake me up (literally and figuratively). The burning in my hands and feet feels like a sweet release of false beliefs. In the sacred stillness of the darkness, I can detach from old stories and simply experience the intensity of emotion seeping from my cells. While disruptive, I'm getting up in the morning with a greater spaciousness within and a deeper capacity to receive whatever Life has to teach me.

Life has a lot to teach you, honey.

As I liberate my layers, I feel more connected to the fairies and to the nature within and all around me. I've been exploring new portals, beyond the time and space continuum, in my own backyard.

Your backyard is a sanctuary for your soul. Your trees are becoming your dearest friends.

Red and Heart. I'm building another trine with them.

The power of three.

Yesterday, I was planting my spring garden with my friend Haley. She asked about you…and I remembered your ashes still in the mineral supplement bag, sitting beside your vision board in my family room.

You and Haley knew what to do…

We poured you into our palms and then sprinkled you across the freshly composted garden bed. On my hands and knees, I kneaded you into the soil. I paused to examine your signature on my wrist…

Love…Me

And realized the "M" in "Me" was starting to fade.

Nothing is permanent, but Love, honey.

I really am absorbing you, Mom. But there was a sadness in that moment. A grasping for what was…

Be gentle with yourself, Nicki Beans. You will always miss your mama…and Life will continue to dip you into the archives of your humanity.

Still on my hands and knees, in a posture of surrender, I tended to the weeds of the garden, the weeds of my mind. As I watched Haley place each tiny seed in the soil, I wanted to be the seed. I wanted Haley's nurturing hands to cover me up with you. I wanted to rest in the quiet peace of the Earth.

Two years ago, we planted the seed of this book with the compost of our stories. We've been tending this garden with Love and Truth, allowing the seed to rest in the dark and prepare for its awakening to the Light. And now, our little seed is pushing its way through the earth of us.

It's ready to bloom, Mom. It's time.

•••

I just glanced at the clock. It's 11:11. You taught me to pay attention when an eleven, the number symbolizing spiritual mastery, reveals itself. As if it's saying, "Yes, dear one, this is the way…"

On our journey through the seasons, honey, we found the way. The way to everywhere and nowhere at once.

By telling our stories and shining Light on the layers of Truth that exist across lifetimes, we can now see that everything is just a sacred prop in the play of Life, an aid for our soul's awakening into extraordinary nothingness.

These dialogues have liberated you, honey. Your essence can now flow freely through your form.

While I have been reliving the dreams of lifetimes, I've also been waking up from them.

You're learning to hold both the humanity and Divinity of your existence. The work now is stay alert and recognize when you've been pulled back into the world of drama and illusion.

When I need to rediscover the stillness behind noise.

Never forget the wisdom that is always waiting for you on the altar of your soul.

I began this project to heal, Mom. I needed to channel you every day, to be reassured of your presence. And certain messages had to be in your voice in order for them to be true.

But now, you are no longer a child who needs her mother. As you have rebirthed yourself, you have also begun the process of dissolving yourself. No more seeking, Nicki Beans. No more thinking, just relax and unfold into the Life that is you.

Enjoy living on this great planet of possibility, honey. Lean into the seasons, the cycles, the circles. Get naked with the water, air, fire and earth of you. Be the ceremony, the moving meditation, the sacred prayer.

Shine your extraordinary Light, baby girl.

I will, Mom. With your smile on my face…

…and Mr. Bluebird on your shoulder…

Let's ALL sing together…

"Zip-a-dee-doo-dah, zip-a-dee-ay
My, oh my, what a wonderful day
Plenty of sunshine headin' my way
Zip-a-dee-doo-dah, zip-a-dee-ay!"

•••

Gratitude for Oakley

•••

My mirror, my medicine, my muse…carrying me on a breeze through the seasons, reminding me over and over again of Life's sweet spiral. I wrap my arms around you, covering only a fraction of your expanse. Mom embraces you from the other side. I can feel her fingers meeting mine. I plant my feet beside you, allowing my roots to tangle with yours. I raise my eyes to marvel at your eternal reach, fading into the Heavens above. A single leaf cascades from a place unseen, a memory of your life after life after life. You summoned my mom to you on a cool October day once upon no-time. It was your will that brought her to the land she last called home. And today, I come to you still, writing you across my page, life after life after life…

Thank you, Oakley.

Thank you, Spirit.

Thank you, Mom.

Final Gratitude

...

This book was made manifest through meditation, intensive soul inquiry, and the transmission of energy and wisdom from amazing teachers and healers. So much gratitude for this circle of humans, my angels on Earth:

Cynthia Bischoff, Jeffrey Boynton, Gailynn Carroll, **Tracey Degregory**, Terry Frank, Lorraine Goldbloom, Alicia Golden, Faith Grieger, Irene Kendig, Samantha Lane, Kush Love, Maggie Macilvaine, Joni Maher, Mary Mayer, Boo Rigsby, Daniel Rigsby, suzanne l. vinson, Cynthia Wallace, Ric Weinman, Kelly Wolf, and the Bounce Collective.

To my guide… Thank you, Merlin/Shine.

And thank you to the artists of the music and poetry that have inspired our lives and the pages of this book...

The Carpenters for "Top of the World"
Chicago for "Hard Habit to Break"
Matthew Wilder and Kobalt Music for "Break My Stride"
Naomi Shihab Nye for her poem "Kindness"
Grace Peasley for her poem "Beginnings"

Zip-A-Dee-Doo-Dah
from SONG OF THE SOUTH
Words by Ray Gilbert
Music by Allie Wrubel
(c) 1945 Walt Disney Music Company
Copyright Renewed.
All Rights Reserved. Used by Permission.
Reprinted by Permission of Hal Leonard LLC

love...
me

Made in the USA
Middletown, DE
25 July 2018